FIRE THE LANDSCAPER

How Landscapers, HOAs, and Cultural Norms
Are Poisoning Our Properties

By

Phil M. Williams

ISBN: 978-1-943894-00-0

Third Printing, 2018
Phil Williams Consulting, LLC.
www.PhilWBooks.com

Contents

A Note From Phil

Dear Reader,

If you're interested in receiving my novel *Against the Grain* for free, and/or reading my other titles for free or discounted, go to the following link: http://www.PhilWBooks.com.
You're probably thinking, *What's the catch?* There is no catch.

Sincerely,
Phil M. Williams

Introduction

In this book I prove the psychological, economic, and cultural reasons for why we maintain our properties the way we do. I use research data, and personal experiences in the landscape industry and as an ecological designer, to shed a light on the extensive damage being done to our ecosystem. I give practical advice on how to improve the health of your property without spending a dime or expending an ounce of energy.

I had an insider's view into the suburban wasteland of the Washington, DC, metropolitan area that boasts five of the top six wealthiest counties in the nation.[1] In the past, as a landscape contractor and proud owner of my very own McMansion, I was part of the problem. It took walking away, some soul searching, plus learning ecological design, permaculture, and organic gardening to understand the devastation that lies beneath our feet.

I hope by pointing out the ridiculous cultural norms inflicted on homeowners—and the equally ridiculous laws enforced by HOAs and local governments—that I might contribute to the

---

1 "List of Highest-Income Counties in the United States," *Wikipedia* (2014), http://en.wikipedia.org/wiki/List_of_highest-income_counties_in_the_United_States.

movement toward healthier food, a healthier environment, and more freedom. At the very least I've enjoyed poking fun at the status quo.

Want to know more about my story? Read Chapter 1 to find out how the "American Dream" almost destroyed my soul.

1

IT'S TIME TO MOVE ON

In 1997 I held a worthless degree in sociology and two jobs, neither paying more than seven dollars an hour. I had been working for a mowing service for only two weeks, but I already hated it. It was a twelve-hour-a-day grind in the Virginia heat, almost jogging behind mowers that were sped up to increase efficiency. I was in decent shape, a former two-sport college athlete, but I came home each day exhausted.

During my long days of hearing nothing but the roar of the mower, I calculated how much money I was making for my employer. Based on my take-home pay, I could mow three lawns a day and equal my salary. My foreman and I were mowing thirty per day between the two of us.

I had the bright idea to take the job I hated and make it a career. A friend of mine from high school was working as a bartender, but he had experience working on a golf course. We decided to print up some flyers and canvass a few neighborhoods while advertising our new mowing service. Our fledgling company was marginally successful that first year, but we did collect twenty-five clients. We didn't know it then, but we were about to ride the biggest housing bubble the world has ever known.

The rocketlike rise from a struggling mowing service in 1997 to a five-million-dollar company took only eight years. I became almost numb to the wealth. In the summer of 2005, I looked like the picture of success. I was the president and majority owner of a successful landscape company. My wife and I had recently moved into a 1.4 million-dollar home in Fairfax Station, Virginia, a suburb of Washington, DC. I was twenty-nine years old and miserable. What was wrong with me?

I became someone who I no longer respected. I did exactly what 99% of Americans would do if they became wealthy: I bought the mansion. I had the home theater, the nice cars, the motorcycle, the gourmet kitchen, and all the trappings of polite society. It's easy for people to rationalize what they do and how they live if everyone around them validates their choices. I tried to rationalize it, but something gnawed at my insides, like a worker bee chewing through the candy cork at the end of a queen cage.

I couldn't be a shallow, materialistic person *and* be happy. My wife says that I'm a minimalist at heart. I often go years without buying new clothes. I drive a thirteen-year-old car. I have no interest in shopping whatsoever. I could live happily in a one-room cabin. My materialism and greed were a departure from my core values. I wasn't proud of who I had become. This identity crisis sent me into a deep depression.

I've struggled with bouts of depression throughout my life. I remember a particularly dark time as a nineteen-year-old, when I was living day to day. I thought, *if things don't get better today, I'll end it tonight.*

This ritual went on for months. It was comforting to think that I could end the pain at any point. I'm not sure if I would have had the "courage" to go through with it, but I do know that, if suicide were as simple as flipping a light switch, I wouldn't be writing this today.

My wife, Denise, was worried. She encouraged me to see a therapist. I was dismayed when the therapist diagnosed me with dysthymia after only one session. Dysthymia is a state of chronic depression, less acute than a major depressive disorder, but long lasting—often two years or more. When things were bad, it was difficult to get out of bed, and, even when things were good, the specter of depression still loomed over me.

It doesn't take a genius to realize that these problems originate in childhood. I took the ACE (Adverse Childhood Experiences) test and scored a five out of ten.[2] The results were alarming because people who score four or higher are subject to much higher risks of social, emotional, and health problems. Compared to someone with a zero score, I am 240% more likely to contract hepatitis, 390% more likely to contract chronic pulmonary lung disease, 600% more likely to beat my wife, 500% more likely to be an alcoholic, 460% more likely to be depressed, and 1220% more likely to commit suicide.[3] Many of my adverse childhood experiences stemmed from growing up with a sociopath.

It is estimated that one in twenty-five Americans are sociopathic.[4] It is a common misconception that sociopaths are collecting heads in their basements or saving body parts in their freezers. While serial killers are most likely sociopaths, most sociopaths never kill anyone. They are simply people who have no conscience. These people can and will do things for their own personal gain or amusement to the detriment of others—without feeling an ounce of remorse.

Most sociopaths waltz through life undetected, secretly

2 Jane Stevens, "What's Your ACE Score?" *ACES Too High* (November 2011), http://acestoohigh.com/got-your-ace-score/.

3 Ibid.

4 Martha Stout, *The Sociopath Next Door*, (New York: Broadway Books, 2005), 6.

wreaking havoc in the lives of those around them. They are notoriously difficult to detect. They've spent a lifetime learning to cover their tracks. Sociopaths are people nonetheless, and they are very different in their behaviors. Martha Stout, PhD, the author of *The Sociopath Next Door*, indicated that, despite their differences, preying on others' sympathies was the most common technique used to conceal their true nature.[5]

I've learned some powerful life lessons from a sociopath. My editor advised me not to disclose the identity of this person for fear of litigation. The original draft of this book contained the person's identity. My initial attitude was, "To hell with them. It's all true." A cooler head prevailed when I thought about what this person is capable of. I am, after all, talking about a sociopath. From here on out I'll refer to this person with the pseudonym, Don, even though he may or may not be male.

Don is a shopaholic and a manipulative liar. His materialism and dishonesty had the opposite effect on me. I was always a frugal and honest child. When I was twelve, I remember saving over $500 from birthdays and chores. I asked Don to hold the money for me, because I was worried about losing it on a vacation. That money was never returned. When I asked for it back, he acted as if it never existed.

I only mention this because I would be remiss not to acknowledge the important influence Don had on my life. I'm not sure I would have made the choices detailed in this book without him. Growing up with a shopaholic, sociopathic, pathological liar forces you to make a *Sophie's Choice* of sorts. You can believe the lies, validate him, stay on his good side, and you can reap the rewards of consumerist crap from time to time, and he will fill your head with insincere grand flattery. You also run the risk of being disappointed when Don lets you down at the precise

5   Ibid 107.

moment you need him the most.

The road less traveled, and the one I have embarked on, involves questioning the status quo, and making choices based on facts and evidence. This behavior causes problems. This behavior upsets people, sometimes people you really do care about. Most people prefer to live in a world where what they do and who they are resides safely in the "good" category, even if facts and evidence don't support it.

I couldn't live without truth. My mind literally rebelled with depression if I lived in a way that didn't align with my need for honesty. Imagine being a young child growing up with a sociopath. Don made me skeptical of everything. I wonder how many of the simple concepts espoused in this book would have died on the vine of cultural bias and propaganda if I wasn't able to question the status quo.

I started to question the sustainability of my business in August of 2005 during Hurricane Katrina. We had a fuel shortage in the Northeast, and prices rose sharply. I didn't understand how a storm in the Gulf could affect gas prices in the Northeast. I did some research into energy, and then I did tons more research to try to disprove what I had discovered. That just sent me deeper into the abyss.

I won't go into detail here, because there are so many good books on the fragility of modern society, but I will say that our society is a lot like Don. It's metaphorically maxing out our credit cards, effectively stealing from future generations.

My change didn't happen overnight. I had to do quite a bit of soul searching, but I realized I was not part of the solution. At first, I thought if I just install the right lightbulbs or drive the right fuel-efficient car, I'd be doing my part. It didn't take long to figure out that wasn't remotely sufficient.

I started with the way I lived. What my wife and I called

"home" was a 7,000-square-foot monstrosity built with vinyl and particle board. The brick facing was for show. Everything in it and on it had a lifetime that I would outlive. Without the natural gas pumped in and electricity delivered, the house would be difficult to inhabit. I was also quite the car enthusiast at the time. I had a Subaru Sti that had a $20,000 motor with close to 500 horsepower. It was a rally car for the street. What a colossal waste of money.

My business was no better. We drove around incessantly mowing lawns that needed to be mowed more frequently because we were applying fertilizers that made them grow quicker. Then we were killing "weeds" that actually helped the soil and the ecosystem. No wonder the bees are dying nationwide. On top of that we installed expensive landscapes with the sole purpose of looking good, so people could keep up appearances. My life and my business were drowning in superficiality. I needed something real.

The only real thing in my life was my wife, Denise. She and I talked about these issues often, so she knew how I was feeling. She didn't know yet that I wanted to do something about it. I hadn't said it aloud because it seemed so impulsive. The more I thought about it, the more certain I became. One evening in June of 2007 I broke the news.

When I told Denise that I wanted to sell the "dream house" we had just moved into, along with everything else we had of value, she cried. She thought I was rejecting her, rejecting the life we had built together. She was concerned that I was depressed. For once I wasn't depressed; I was awake. I explained to her how I felt our lifestyle was unsustainable and that our new house would lose value in the future. We talked about leaving our friends and what we might do. She tried to convince me that what I did for a living was good for society because I was an honest businessman who treated his customers and employees fairly.

The following is not my exact response, because I don't remember all that I said, but I did make these points:

> It's easy to rationalize what I do. It's like what Upton Sinclair said. "It is difficult to get a man to understand something when his salary depends on his not understanding it." I'm looking at myself and my business objectively. What do we really do? We drive around burning valuable nonrenewable fuel to cut lawns far too frequently. We apply chemicals to the lawns so they grow faster, and then we need to cut them more often. We kill every last "weed" in sight with some chemicals that can remain in the soil for one hundred years. And those supposed weeds are there to improve the soil. My clients bitch if they have a single clover or dandelion in their yard. Did you know that clover fixes nitrogen and attracts pollinators? Dandelions help aerate the soil, accumulate nutrients, and they can be eaten. We plant trees and shrubs that have no purpose other than aesthetics. And for what? So my clients can keep up with the Joneses?

Denise is a very rational person with an open mind. The more she learned, the more she loved the idea of getting out of suburbia and trying to live a simpler, more sustainable life. However, she wasn't quite as confident that it was a good idea to walk away and live off the land because I was inspired by Thoreau. She was right that people don't live like *Little House on the Prairie* anymore for a reason. Of course, this was all just talk at this point. We ended the discussion agreeing to put the house on the market to see what would happen. I told her that I didn't think we'd be able to sell it. I was wrong.

I sold my car first; that was easy. I got about as much for the car as I had put into the motor. Then I paid our tenants in our rental house to leave, so I could get that house on the market. Within three months of putting the houses up for sale, they were sold. I priced them low enough to sell quickly, because I considered, if I priced them too high, the falling market would ultimately yield a lower price down the road. We lost $200,000 on our new house, but we made about that on the old one.

The business sale was much trickier. I had a conversation with a landscape industry consultant, and I mentioned off-the-cuff that I would walk away from my business for the right price. Shortly thereafter he came to me with a prospective buyer. After some negotiation they offered a price acceptable to me. I told my business partner that, if we sold, we could do an even split, even though I was the majority owner. He decided to borrow the money to buy me out.

Leaving my company gave me the time to figure out how to live and work without compromising my ideals. I spent the subsequent seven years researching and trying everything from building science, weatherization, alternative energy, carpentry, organic gardening, food preservation, animal husbandry, beekeeping, excavating, pond building, gray water, forestry, and maintenance.

Ultimately, I discovered a system of design that incorporated sustainable systems and skills from the traditional to the modern. I'm convinced this design science can revolutionize how properties are developed and maintained across the urban, suburban, and rural landscapes of the world. In this book, I prove the folly of our currently accepted landscape design and maintenance practices, and provide practical alternatives to drastically improve the health of your property and the environment at large. I hope you will set aside your cultural biases and read this book with an open mind.

In the next chapter I'll address the advent of the grass lawn.

2

ORIGINS OF THE GRASS LAWN

In 1540 the word "laune" was related to the Celtic word "lan" which means "enclosure."[6] So, "laune" was used to describe communal grass enclosures for grazing livestock. This may be where the term "lawn" originated.[7] These large expanses were usually owned by a British aristocrat who rented the land to a tenant farmer to graze.

Lawns in the Middle Ages grew in northern Europe. The cool, damp weather in the area made lawns conceivable. The aristocracy of the time had the surplus wealth to provide for the maintenance. Before the advent of mechanical mowers, lawns were maintained with grazing animals or with scythes.[8] Horses and sheep, grazed regularly, can give the low-cut "lawn" appearance without the modern mower. By the eighteenth century, the closely cropped English lawn became a status symbol.[9]

As stuck-up as that sounds, the old-time English lawn was downright sustainable when compared to the energy and

6 "Lawn," *Wikipedia* (2016), http://en.wikipedia.org/wiki/Lawn.
7 Ibid.
8 Ibid.
9 Ibid.

resource sinks we cultivate today. The English lords of the time used the space for grazing, did not deploy harmful chemicals, and allowed a mixture of meadow plants.

In eighteenth century America, the plague of the grass lawn was imported by the wealthy. Thomas Jefferson was one of the early adopters with his attempt of a lawn at Monticello.[10] By the nineteenth century, industrialization, the production of the lawn mower, and suburbanization had sealed our fate. The lawn was now within the grasp of the middle class. It didn't hurt that the United States was the world's largest producer of oil. What started as a status symbol became an entrenched aesthetic in our built landscapes, fueled by the desire to leave our agricultural roots to the dwindling farmers and to escape the heavy pollution in our cities. The middle class and the wealthy moved to the suburbs in droves.

The grass lawn and the associated industries boomed until the Great Depression. With the Great Depression biting, people struggled to keep up appearances. Lawn care suppliers, such as The Scotts Miracle-Gro Company, encouraged Americans to continue maintaining their useless patches of grass, touting the work as stress-relieving. During World War II, homeowners were again expected to keep up appearances as a show of strength and unity.[11] After the war, with the GI Bill helping veterans purchase new homes in the 'burbs, the lawn reasserted its dominance as the central landscape feature over the vast majority of the United States.[12]

What started as envy grew into vanity and matured as a cultural convention. Today the lawn is so pervasive in our society that we force people to not only have lawns but to maintain them at a certain height and uniformity.

10 Ibid.

11 Ibid.

12 Ibid.

- In the Middle Ages, British aristocrats grew lawns for grazing.
- By the eighteenth century the closely cropped English lawn became a status symbol.
- Industrialization and the production of the gas-powered lawn mower made the lawn affordable to the masses.
- Cultural convention has kept lawns popular and even legally mandated (by some HOAs and local laws—more on that later), despite their uselessness and the damage to the environment caused by their upkeep.

Chapter 3 shows how Mother Nature does her landscaping. Note how it is different from what we are taught to do.

3

MOTHER NATURE NEVER STOPS, THE STORY OF SUCCESSION

Mother Nature abhors a vacuum. Give her an empty niche, and she'll undoubtedly fill it. She always has an eye toward the future, and she knows exactly how to get there. You can fight her all the way, but, in the end, you'll tire and whither, and she'll win.

Much of North America would revert back to forest if humans stopped mowing, spraying, chainsawing, plowing, and pruning. The Midwest would return to prairie land if they stopped using mechanized combines and cultivators to produce monoculture corn and soy crops. Parts of Texas would become a savanna of large animals grazing a landscape with drought-tolerant trees and shrubs as a sparse tree canopy.

In Central Pennsylvania where I reside, we have good loam soil, a generous rainfall amount close to fifty inches annually, and a temperate climate. Mother Nature desperately wants a forest to be here. If I were to clear my property, strip all the vegetation, and simply walk away, succession would begin immediately.

Quick-germinating annual and perennial herbaceous weeds would appear first. These "weeds" would begin the healing process from any damage I caused. These early pioneers begin the process of creating the conditions for a forest to thrive. These "weeds" are particularly adept at quickly covering bare earth. Their job is to shield the earth from erosion and to mine nutrients from deep in the soil to make them more readily available.[13]

Pioneer weeds—such as plantain, dandelion, and chicory—make great nutrient miners because they have long tap roots. These three weeds also make great edibles for people, animals, and insects alike. To top it off, the dandelion is one of the best early season nectar sources for bees, and the chicory at my home blooms from June until November, providing a long-lasting source of nectar.

Shortly after the quick-germinating pioneers, larger perennial weeds will begin to take hold. While the pioneers will still thrive, the typically taller perennials will begin to shade them and dominate the site. Here you'll see flourishing perennial grasses—clover, goldenrod, bindweed, and thistle.[14] These weeds will create more biomass, which is crucial to building soil and life. Some perennial weeds, such as clover, will draw in nitrogen from the atmosphere. Clover provides that necessary element to the soil when the plant is cut, eaten, or when it dies back in the winter. The increased size and diversity of the perennials adds to the soil, insect, and animal life.

Fast-growing pioneer shrubs and trees begin to dominate the site after about five years of neglect.[15] These plants are often nitrogen fixers, such as alder, black locust, or mimosa. Just as often they are simply creating biomass and fast carbon pathways, like the dreaded tree of heaven or the chokecherry.

13 Toby Hemenway, *Gaia's Garden* (White River Junction, VT: Chelsea Green Publishing Company, 2009), 24-26.

14 Ibid.

15 Ibid.

The tree of heaven—or its slang versions: the stink tree, ghetto palm, and tree of hell—is an import from China that has the unique ability to grow vigorously on damaged sites with terrible fertility. These trees are universally hated for their smell of cat urine, plus their vigorous spreading nature, allelopathy (suppressing the growth of nearby plant species), not to mention these trees' general uselessness. One thing tree-of-heaven haters don't realize is that the tree is short lived and doesn't persist in a mature forest. It is another item in Mother Nature's tool box to fix the destruction we've caused.

Having said that, I don't like the tree much either, but I allow the males (which don't produce seed) to exist as windbreaks, animal habitats, and privacy screenings on the outer edges of my six-acre property. The tree has been used successfully to reveg-etate some of the most degraded hilltops in West Virginia after coal mining operations. Like the perennial and annual "weeds" mentioned before, the pioneer trees and shrubs add even more biomass while living and then shedding woody parts and leaves, not to mention the increased diversity and niches created by their existence and by-products.

After a few decades, the short-lived pioneer trees will start to give way to the larger climax species. Eventually my land will have a forest dominated by species such as white pines, oaks, chestnuts, hickory, tulip poplar, black gums, and maples. I will still find the short-lived pioneers on the edges and where open-ings in the upper forest canopy appear, but their dominance will be no more.[16]

Mother Nature is determined to have her forest, no matter how hard we work on our lawns. We can mow, but the grass never stops growing. No matter how many chemicals we spray, "weeds" continue to appear. We work so hard to keep our landscapes in

16 Ibid.

a perpetual state of immature succession, but Mother Nature is patient. She'll have her forest only a few decades after we give up.[17]

Our expertly maintained landscapes that suburbanites spend a fortune on are nothing more than immature, polluted, artificial representations of nature. These properties speed up the succession process with fertilizers and irrigation systems, but then slam on the brakes of succession with constant mowing, weeding, and herbicide use. We have created synthetic landscapes with an identity crisis.[18]

Our valuable time and resources are squandered to maintain our landscapes in a perpetual state of immaturity. When I drive through a neighborhood with underground sprinkler systems, diagonally striped "perfect" lawns, neatly clipped shrubs, and mulch without a single "weed," I don't see beauty; I see a wasteland filled with ignorance and hubris.

- Much of North America would revert back to forest if humans stopped interfering.

- When we mow, prune, chainsaw, and spray herbicides, we keep our landscapes in a perpetual state of immaturity.

- Our expertly maintained landscapes that suburbanites spend a fortune on are nothing more than immature, polluted, artificial representations of nature.

In the next chapter you'll see the wisdom of Mother Nature over our contemporary golf-course-lawn mentality.

---

17 Ibid.
18 Ibid.

4

MONOCULTURE VERSUS POLYCULTURE

"Monoculture" is the cultivation of a single crop in a given area. The large acreages of corn, soy, and wheat fields that dominate our agricultural systems would be an example of this. These monoculture systems allow for mechanical cultivation and harvesting but are heavily reliant on fossil fuels, irrigation, and chemicals to maintain them.

"Polyculture" is the cultivation of multiple crops in a given area. The Native American "three sisters' garden" of corn, beans, and squash grown together is considered a polyculture system. In this system the corn acts as a trellis for the beans, and dappled shade for the squash. The beans provide nitrogen fixation for the corn and squash. The squash acts as a ground cover, providing weed control, protecting the soil from erosion, and confusing the corn worms. Monoculture dominates our maintained landscapes, but polyculture reigns supreme in our natural systems.

The manicured, chemically treated grass lawn is the epitome of monoculture. Our society has embraced the "golf course" lawn as a standard worth striving for. As a landscaper, I had thousands of clients who contracted with my business for our lawn treatment program. The program included ten treatments, a fall aeration and seed, and slit seeding for all those bare spots that develop over the summer. It bothered me that the lawns my company cared for were less resilient than lawns where we simply mowed every two weeks.

In order to maintain that perfect monoculture, we had to provide all the needs of that system. We had to provide the fertilizer, as we made sure to kill all the nitrogen-fixing and nutrient-accumulating plants with our weed treatments. We had to provide constant weed, disease, and insect control, because we were working against nature to keep the lawn in an immature monoculture state of succession. If our clients didn't water heavily in the summer, you can guarantee their yard would be among the first to brown.

Meanwhile, our clients who did nothing to their yards, except mow infrequently, still had healthy green lawns. While they did have a mixture of weeds, that diversity was the key to a green, yet low-maintenance yard. In the summer, without irrigation, these untreated polycultured lawns succumbed to dormancy much later than my unirrigated properties on the treatment program. On my irrigated lawns, the common turf disease, suitably named *brown patch*, needed constant fungicide sprays, or the grass could have severe outbreaks. My untreated yards never had enough disease to notice.

Without insect control treatments, specifically grub control, my treated lawns ran the risk of terrible infestations. I've visited properties where you could pull the grass back, like carpet, because the roots had been decimated by white grubs. With the diversity of species in the untreated lawns, insects were never a problem.

Monoculture Chemically Treated Lawn Complete with Pesticide Warning Sign

Lawns could be transformed from monoculture resource sinks into low-maintenance ground covers simply by stopping the treatments and reducing the mowing frequency to twice per month. This will allow nature to grow the plants necessary to repair the damage done to the soil. Clover, dandelions, plantains, crabgrass, orchard grass, wood sorrel, and many other plant species will create the polyculture diversity needed to restore balance and health to your property. The benefit to you will be much less work, better soil, better pollination, more natural beauty, more diversity, edible herbs growing, and an ecosystem safe enough to eat from.

If you'd prefer a diverse lawn of your choosing, the polyculture diversity can be mimicked and seeded with many different beneficial herbs and grasses, such as chamomile, creeping thyme, Dutch white clover, purslane, English daisy, and many others.

Why would anyone choose a boring, toxic, expensive, mono-cultured lawn when you could have a diverse, healthy, edible, blooming, low-maintenance meadow?

Monoculture is not unique to our chem-lawns. The over-priced landscapes especially pervasive in suburbia exhibit similar monoculture qualities. Hedgerows of evergreen shrubs tend to hug foundations, while lines of perennial flowers or smaller blooming deciduous shrubs are in front. Mostly these landscapes are mulched with a bark or wood material. The occasional tree dots the landscape with the same mulch formed in a ring. While the diversity is better for the typical front-yard foundation planting, it is still very monocultured in that many like species are next to each other. Also, there is no thought placed into arranging plants similar to the three sisters' garden, where certain species are grouped together based on their beneficial coexistence.

If you observe nature, you will find many plants that coexist with certain other plant species, like a tribe or a guild. Polyculture guilds are groupings of plants that benefit each other. These plants are stronger as part of a guild than on their own. Nature can be recreated in our designed landscapes to save energy, work, and increase the quality of plant health. No longer will we be forced to provide all the necessities demanded of a monoculture. In a polyculture guild, Mother Nature lends a helping hand.[19]

For example, my fruit trees are the centerpiece of a polyculture guild. Along with each fruit tree, I like to plant comfrey, which is a great nutrient accumulator to help reduce the need for fertilizer. It also produces an abundance of nutrient-rich leaves that can be cut periodically and spread around the fruit trees as mulch. Comfrey is also a pollinator favorite with its beautiful purple flowers. To top it off, comfrey makes a great salve for injuries and can even be used to inoculate compost piles.

19 Ibid, 177-180.

Polyculture Guild: Plum with Goumi, Comfrey, Milkweed, Clover, Alfalfa, Oregano, Yarrow

Along with comfrey, I love to plant dill and yarrow under the trees. The small flowers these plants produce are favorites of beneficial insect predators, such as ladybugs, hoverflies, and lacewings. By creating the environment where beneficial insects thrive, insect damage to trees and fruit is reduced. I usually round out my fruit tree guilds with a couple of nitrogen fixers. I like to use *goumi*, which is a nitrogen-fixing shrub that produces an edible berry.

In addition to adding to the soil's fertility, *goumi* provides wildlife habitat for our feathered friends. Birds are excellent at reducing worm populations and providing fertilizer in place. To finish the duo of fertility builders, my favorite guild plant is undoubtedly clover. Clover is a nitrogen fixer, an excellent living mulch, and is one of the best nectar sources available for pollinators and beneficial insects alike.

- Monoculture is the cultivation of a single crop in a given area.

- Polyculture is the cultivation of multiple crops in a given area.

- A monoculture system needs many outside inputs, such as chemicals and petroleum, to be productive.

- In a polyculture system, the diversity of plants helps to provide for the needs of the system.

Next, I cover the importance of questioning our cultural norms.

5

OUR OBSESSION WITH ORDER
AND CONFORMITY

It amazes me the extent to which people who reside in the developed world can exist almost entirely outside of nature. Most Americans live in climate-controlled homes, where they don't have to experience the heat of summer or the bite of winter. When we leave our homes, we go directly to climate controlled cars. We even have automatic starters, so we don't have to wait for the car to heat up or cool down. We travel to offices, restaurants, and shopping centers, all destinations with perfectly maintained year-round temperatures. Children stay inside far more often with electronics as a constant source of entertainment.

I believe this gradual disconnection from nature, occurring since the Industrial Revolution, has contributed to our obsession with order and conformity in our landscapes.

I had a client in an upscale Virginia suburb who was deathly afraid of insects. He wanted us to remove every plant on his property, thinking that, without plants, there would be no insects. He was okay with keeping the grass, but he said, if the HOA would allow it, he'd concrete his entire property. He insisted on a weed barrier and rocks against the house. He had a pest control company come in every few weeks and spray the perimeter with insecticide. If it was alive, he wanted it dead!

I contracted with this client to remove all the vines, shrubs, and flowers from his property. One Monday before his job was scheduled, we had a cancellation, and I needed work for my crew to do, or I'd have to send them home. This man's job, although not scheduled yet, was perfect to fit in, as it required no materials or calls to locate utilities. We showed up that Monday morning unannounced. A little after 8:00 a.m. the crew started to cut down his azaleas in the front yard. He came barreling out of his house, red-faced, in his shorts and T-shirt.

I was in my truck about to pull away, when I saw him. I immediately got out of my vehicle and met him in the middle of the yard. I knew this was my bullet to take, not the crew's. He proceeded to scream at me for my incompetence. He was upset that we had showed up unannounced, running our chain saws in the morning. I apologized and offered to have the crew hold off on any noisy work until it was okay with him.

He pointed to his two BMWs in the driveway and said, "I have to go to work to pay for those. I don't have time for this today."

I humbly apologized, and I sent the crew to my house to do some work, so they wouldn't miss a day's pay. The point of this story is not to show that this guy was an arrogant ass or that I should have called. Both of those things are true, but, more important, this guy was angry, and he wanted control. He didn't really care about the noise. Everyone in his house had been up since six o'clock.

He cared that I didn't ask him for permission to be there that morning. He had two young children and a timid wife, but he wasn't concerned about the unnatural environment his family was living in. He *was* concerned about his BMWs and putting the landscaper firmly in his place. A big part of understanding

Mother Nature is learning to let go of the modern notion that we have control; we don't.

As a teenager, I lived in a Virginia suburb of DC. We had a quarter-acre lot, with many mature hardwoods in the backyard. These trees were over fifty feet tall and produced tons of leaves. Every weekend throughout the fall, my dad would make my brother and me hand-rake every last leaf, place them in plastic bags, and deposit the bags on the curb. He used to count the bags of leaves.

"We bagged eighty-seven this week!" he said with pride.

For me, it was miserable, tedious work that seemed pointless. The raking wasn't that bad, but actually depositing all those leaves into bags was ridiculous. We spent every weekend for those two months raking leaves. The result was that the soil underneath was compacted and grew very little of anything.

Those leaves we removed were a fantastic mulch that nature provides free of charge. That mulch eventually becomes compost and fertilizer for the trees. We wasted 8 weekends, 16 days, and approximately 256 man-hours per year making the soil worse, stealing nutrients from those trees, and putting great organic material into plastic bags.

What was the point? The only reason was to conform to the cultural norms of neatness and orderliness. My dad is a smart guy, a West Point graduate. Why didn't he ask why? It was just assumed that this was the right thing to do. There was *never* any question. I believe our society and education system teaches us facts and figures, and how to do things, but it does not teach us to question cultural norms. If anything, it teaches us to worship the status quo and belittle those who strike at accepted norms.

Later in life, when I became a landscaper, those norms were still firmly entrenched. I had thousands of clients who paid my company to remove leaves under trees, only to pay us again to replace the leaves with wood mulch.

In the United States the cultural norm is to have a grass lawn without "weeds" and some nonedible plants, neatly clipped, growing around the foundation of the house in brown mulch. How many people actually ask why? Or question is this the best thing for my property? I explained in Chapter 2 how we got here, but why do we continue to do something that is so obviously ignorant? Once a practice is widely accepted in society, it is very difficult to change.

Cultural norms are like large cruise ships. It requires a tremendous amount of force to turn them just a little. Our human need to be accepted, to belong, to be part of a group is extremely strong. We've evolved as a tribal society where going it alone meant certain death and where going against the norms of your tribe could mean banishment. It makes sense to me that we still hold

Typical Monoculture Lawn with Foundation Plantings

on to those genetic needs of acceptance, no matter how irrational they might be. The need to be accepted is so strong that those who are socially ostracized often suffer depression. This physical and emotional need to belong creates a slow-moving herd nearly impossible to reason with to effect a change in direction.

On top of our genetic need to conform, we have to break through confirmation biases to change tightly held beliefs. "Confirmation bias" is the tendency to interpret and pursue information that confirms one's beliefs. Social media is a haven for confirmation bias. People like and dislike news, information, and pictures based on their beliefs. Before they know it, their social media feeds are echo chambers with little to no open and honest discussions. You can easily test this theory. Comment critically on your Republican friend's pro-Trump article, or your Democrat friend's pro-Obama article. Chances are other people that are in their herd will refute your claims with fervor. Many people are offended by disagreement because they've insulated themselves with likeminded individuals, and the uncommon disagreement now feels rude and distressing.

Confirmation bias tends to be more of a problem when people are emotionally connected to the belief or when it enhances their self-esteem. If you confront a conformist with conflicting information, they will often hold even tighter to their original belief. Many of these biases were developed in childhood, when they were propagandized without the means to resist. This is one reason why smart people can hold faulty opinions and beliefs.

> *Smart people believe weird things because they are skilled at defending beliefs they arrived at for nonsmart reasons.*
>
> —Michael Shermer

I don't think confirmation bias is directly causal to the way we maintain properties because confirmation biases tend to center on more emotional issues. I do think confirmation bias contributes greatly to our attitude toward the environment in general, which contributes to our unnatural landscapes. Global warming, climate change, or whatever you want to call it is a hot-button issue that triggers a tremendous amount of confirmation bias.

Typically, you have conservative Republican types denying the issue and liberal Democrats on the other side. These individuals on both sides of the aisle often come to these conclusions—not because of open-minded research but biased information from their "trusted" news source. This also boosts their self-esteem and places them in the warm embrace of their particular herd.

Whether you are a believer in anthropogenic (human-caused) global warming or not, does not matter in my opinion. Anyone who has looked out the window of an airplane can very easily see how we have cleared forests and sculpted the land into endless square plots of monoculture farming, suburban tract homes, and strip malls. With only a cursory amount of research you can find credible information about the increase in desertification; the pollution of fresh and salt water alike; the depletion of mineral resources; and the loss of fisheries, diversity, and topsoil.

If you simply open your eyes to the natural world, it's plain as day. This is the problem with the global warming debate. It's too esoteric. It's hard for people to do something when the problem is complicated and fraught with misinformation and bias. Mother Nature, on the other hand, is right in front of us; we just have to see her.

Coming from a disciplined, conformist, military household—and spending a decade in the landscape industry—certainly instilled plenty of biases in me. I'm not special in that regard. I didn't wake up one day and realize my beliefs were shrouded in culture and bias. Like most, I thought I had made decisions based on logic, reason, and science.

The big change for me was when I started to ask *Why?* and *Why not?* I started to question everything that goes unquestioned. I was desperately searching for truth. I wondered how many of my decisions were really of my own volition. Did I favor the United States because it's the best country in the world or because I was born here and influenced by the media, government schools, American culture, and even my friends and family? Are devout Christians making a conscious choice? What if they grew up in Pakistan? In that scenario they'd likely be devout Muslims. Human beings have had propaganda and cultural biases rammed down their throats since birth. Most go through life affirming and regurgitating their brand of misinformation comfortably among the like-minded.

- Cultural norms are difficult to change because human beings have a biological need to conform.

- Through confirmation bias, people tend to interpret and pursue information that confirms their beliefs.

- Many biases were developed in childhood, when people were propagandized without the means to resist.

Now that we've identified how individuals and societies can engage in self-destructive thinking and habits that damage our environment, plus cost us time and money, let's move on to the dangers of pesticides.

6

PESTICIDE TOXICITY

As a landscaper, I held a commercial pesticide applicator's license. I sprayed thousands of lawns, designed our company's lawn and plant treatment programs, and trained many of our technicians over the years. I knew that spraying those chemicals wasn't a good thing for the environment, but I felt—because we used some organic fertilizers, and only spot-sprayed herbicides and fungicides—we were doing our part.

Compared to our competitors' usage of fertilizers mixed with herbicides to douse entire yards, whether they had weeds or not, we were doing a good job. Of course, the comparison is faulty, like one burglar feeling morally superior to his thieving friend who happens to steal more often.

Pesticides are everywhere. Our food is sprayed with pesticides (yes, even organic produce), along with our lawns, our landscapes, the cracks of our sidewalks, our clothing, our pools. Our skin is sprayed with bug spray; our homes are doused with household cleaners, and our drinking water contains traces of many pesticides. It's impossible to exist in a pesticide-free world. How dangerous *are* these pesticides?

I started to think about that question in 1999 when I attended a recertification class for my applicator's license. They encouraged us to have cholinesterase tests (for organophosphates) to determine if our body's exposure to the chemicals we were applying was reaching dangerous levels. I thought about how I knew all the different smells of the chemicals I applied. I remember the speaker talking about the dangers of going to the bathroom before washing your hands. He said a common way of ingesting chemicals was for applicators to transmit the poison from their hands through the sensitive skin of their penis.

Any pesticide can be deadly, like many common foods can be deadly; it is just a matter of dosage and how it is ingested. If you drank a glass of window cleaner, you'd be in bad shape; but, if you smelled your window after using the cleaner, you'd be fine. Of course, most people aren't worried about drinking something that we all know is a poison. People are worried about whether or not the food they eat, the water they drink, or the environment they live in may make them or their children sick.

In my research I read the details of over one hundred studies linking different types of cancer and autism to pesticide exposure. I actually started to feel sick to my stomach as I read each study, wondering about my own exposure. I won't rehash the details of every one, as the information is easily searchable here: https://beyondpesticides.org/resources/pesticide-gateway. I will share some important points:

- You are more likely to develop cancer if you have a profession that handles chemicals, such as a pesticide applicator or a farmer.

- There are increased risks for people who live in rural farming communities or near farms.

- There are increased risks for children versus adults.

- Fetuses suffer increased risks of autism and brain tumors if their mothers are exposed to pesticides.

A recent study in the Sacramento Valley revealed that mothers who lived within one mile of fields treated with organophosphate pesticides were 60% more likely to have a child with autism.[20]

My rural community is filled with monoculture chem-ag farms.

However, it's not only farming communities and commercial pesticide applicators that are at risk. A 2010 study, entitled "Childhood Brain Tumors, Residential Insecticide Exposure, and Pesticide Metabolism Genes," suggests that exposure to household insecticides during childhood increases the risk for brain tumors.[21] A 2007 study, entitled "Reported Residential Pesticide Use and Breast Cancer Risk on Long Island, New York," links *residential* use of pesticides in the lawn or garden with increased incidences of breast cancer.[22]

Our friends in the animal kingdom are suffering as well. As a beekeeper and gardener, I am acutely aware of the dangers to bees. Colony collapse disorder or CCD is a syndrome where adult bees simply disappear. A USDA report to Congress indicated that CCD was caused by pest and disease pressures, as well

---

20 Lindsey Konkel, "Autism Risk Higher Near Pesticide-Treated Fields, Study Says," *Environmental Health Sciences* (June 23, 2014), www.environmentalhealthnews.org/ehs/news/2014/jun/autism-and-pesticides.

21 Susan Searles Nielsen, et al, "Childhood Brain Tumors, Residential Insecticide Exposure, and Pesticide Metabolism Genes," *Environmental Health Perspectives* (January, 2010), https://ehp.niehs.nih.gov/0901226/.

22 Susan Teitelbaum, et al, "Reported Residential Pesticide Use and Breast Cancer Risk on Long Island, New York," *American Journal of Epidemiology* (December 13, 2006), http://epiville.ccnmtl.columbia.edu/assets/pdfs/Stellman%20pesticide%20breast%20cancer-1.pdf.

as pesticides.[23] I agree that it's not just one thing killing off the bees. We do have varroa mites, which began plaguing U.S. hives in 1985, and pesticides are certainly a factor, but I think another big problem is the lack of available forage.

Take a drive around your neighborhood in the summer and see if you can find good bee forage. Do your neighbors have clover flowering in their yards? How about dandelions, chicory, or milkweed?

The Author with his Warre Beehives and Shelter

When I drive around my rural community, I see lawns cut so short that, even if they did have good forage, it never has a chance to bloom. I see monoculture farms where thousands of acres are toxic for my bees to even enter. In our quest to dominate "weeds,"

---

23 "Colony Collapse Disorder Progress Report," *USDA* (June, 2010), https://www.ars.usda.gov/is/br/ccd/ccdprogressreport2010.pdf.

we forgot about the insects and animals in the food chain that depend on those plants. A European study conducted in 2012 demonstrated that a microamount of pesticide exposure can cause enough disorientation among bees that they cannot return to their hive.[24] Honeybees are communal; without their hive, they cannot survive.

Aquatic life is especially sensitive to pesticides in the environment. I have four ponds on my property, and it's amazing to see the explosion of life in and around water. Aquatic systems are the most productive known to man, vastly outproducing terrestrial systems in building soil and protein. These robust, diverse systems are particularly susceptible to pesticides, which have been linked to sterility and death involving not only fish but amphibians, mussels, waterbirds, and other wildlife.

A 1992-2001 USGS (US Geological Survey) study found that 57% of stream water in agricultural areas and 83% in urban areas had one or more pesticide compounds that exceeded an aquatic-life benchmark. The benchmark is an estimate of the concentrations of chemicals when, if exceeded, could have adverse effects. In this study at least one pesticide was found in *every* stream they studied.[25]

Our environment is toxic, and people are getting sick. The worst part is that children are the most susceptible. Even with the urban and suburban risks, it's not practical for people to pick up and move to what little pristine wilderness still exists on this planet. The question then becomes, what can we do to increase

24 Mickael Henry, et al, "A Common Pesticide Decreases Foraging Success and Survival in Honeybees," *Science* (April 20, 2012), http://science. sciencemag.org/content/336/6079/348.

25 Gilliom, R., P. Hamilton, "Pesticides in the Nation's Streams and Groundwater, 1992-2001: A Summary," *US Geological Survey* (March, 2006), http://pubs.usgs.gov/fs/2006/3028/.

the health of our local environment?

I had a client recently, who, like many of my clients, was very concerned about the health of herself and her family. She bought organic produce and wanted to grow some of her own food on her half-acre suburban lot. My job was to design the garden. The first thing I noticed was that the lawn was a grass monoculture without a single weed. I asked her if she had a lawn service treating the grass. After she affirmed, I asked her why. She said she didn't want the neighbors to get upset about weeds in her lawn.

My initial thought was *who cares what the neighbors think!*

The first thing we can do to increase the health of our local environment is to stop dumping chemicals on our landscapes. Why on earth would we pay someone to poison our properties? Out of politeness? Out of a desire for uniformity? To conform with our neighbors? This practice is harmful to you, your family, and the environment. Don't be one of those people who can't think for themselves.

- Modern life is filled with chemicals.

- Increased dangers exist for children and the unborn versus adults.

- Increased dangers exist for people who handle chemicals or live near chem-ag farms.

- Bees and aquatic life are suffering because of pesticide exposure.

- A USGS study found that *every* stream tested contained at least one chemical.

The next chapter goes into more details about pesticides and how we can step off the pesticide treadmill.

7

THE PESTICIDE TREADMILL

Proponents of pesticide use would point to the benefits they provide, such as increased yields and labor savings. If pesticides were eliminated tomorrow, farm yields would plummet, and billions of people would starve. Our monoculture chem-ag farms depend on pesticides to operate. Some crop yields would be mostly eliminated. The most pesticide-hungry crop in the United States is the apple.

I imagine it would be near impossible to grow apples without pesticides in the above cold-turkey scenario. The majority of apples would be overtaken by codling moth, apple scab, apple maggot, the apple curculio, or one of the other many diseases and insects that love to attack apple trees. Our society is wholly dependent on pesticides. We are stuck on the pesticide treadmill.

For most of my adult life, I was an advocate for the benefits of pesticides in my business. I rationalized what I did because I profited from it.

Monoculture Chem-Ag Farm

It is difficult to get a man to understand something when his salary depends on his not understanding it.
—Upton Sinclair

I remember telling my sister, who is a devout Whole Foods shopper, that pesticides were good because, otherwise, our food would be inundated with insects. Many years later, when I changed my mind in this regard, she made sure to remind me of my prior folly. I suppose I deserved the chastising.

The idea that pesticides are harmful to your health and the environment was quickly acceptable to me, but I couldn't go cold turkey on them because of the labor savings. I knew it would take ten times longer to hand-weed an area than to simply use an herbicide. When I first started to plant and grow my own fruit trees, a successful local orchardist told me that, without spraying,

I would never get a decent crop. I wanted to stop spraying chemicals, but how could I possibly maintain my large garden and orchard without them?

The concept of the pesticide treadmill finally sold me on the idea that chemicals were not only bad for your health and the environment but they created an unsustainable garden. This concept motivated me to redesign my property and go cold turkey on pesticides. For example, if you notice aphids on your lettuce, and you spray an insecticide, a couple of things happen. The insecticide will kill most of the aphids, but not all. The insecticide will also knock out any aphid predators that may have been trying to help. The predators always come after the prey, and in much smaller numbers, so you may not even know they're there.

The remaining now-pesticide-resistant superaphids that made it through your spraying will breed very rapidly, and, before you know it, you have another outbreak. However, the aphid predators breed slower and are even further behind the increased population of their prey than before you sprayed the first time. So, you have to spray again. You are now on the pesticide treadmill, and it just gets worse over time.

Another example is if you have an unmulched garden with a lot of bare earth. Immediately "weeds" move in because nature is just trying to fix a problem. Seeing these "weeds," you spray and kill them with an herbicide. More weeds continue to show up, which leads to more spraying. The bare earth becomes compacted, because there is no ground cover. Then "weeds" that help fix compacted earth show up, and you kill those as well. The ground is now unsuitable for anything but the sturdiest of weeds. Again, you are on the pesticide treadmill.

I give tours of my home's gardens, and people often ask how I deal with weeds and insects without pesticides. "Healthy soil, better design, and a change of attitude" is my standard answer.

Healthy fertile soil is crucial to growing the high-maintenance vegetables, flowers, and fruit trees that people love. With nitrogen-fixing plants, mulches, composts, and compost teas, we can build healthy soils which will, in turn, build healthy plants. Healthy plants are less likely to be preyed on by pests, therefore negating the need for pesticides.

Most of the trees on my property receive little to no care and they grow well and produce good fruit, but these trees are native nongrafted trees such as mulberries, persimmons, paw paws, elderberries, chockcherries, and native plums. My grafted trees that produce fruit similar to what you might find in a grocery store, do require a bit more care to yield a good crop. I avoid harsh chemicals, but I do spray products like kaolin clay and neem oil. Kaolin clay is exactly that—clay. The tiny clay particles act as a repellant to common pests. Neem oil is a vegetable oil that's made from pressed seeds and fruits of the neem tree. Neem works as an insect repellant and fungicide. I'd love to be super lazy and spray nothing on my trees, but I've found that on the high maintenance fruit trees, I simply won't get a yield. Having said that, I am comfortable with the above products. There's a great book called *The Holistic Orchard* by Michael Phillips that explains how to care for an orchard without harsh chemicals. I've followed his advice with great success.

Designing a garden and landscape that mimics nature and natural plant communities—instead of one designed to look neat and orderly—will also help. For example, many gardeners grow their vegetables in structured rows with similar plants. This setup resembles a grocery store for your pests. Any pests that like a particular plant, fruit, or vegetable will easily go from plant to plant, right down the row. A well-planned polyculture-planted garden with a mixture of many different plants and varieties is confusing for pests.

A confused pest becomes easy prey. Incorporating flowers that provide nectar throughout the season will invite predator insects into the garden to reduce the pests for you. Learning what plants grow best together can create beneficial plant communities where the plants perform better than they would individually.

An attitude adjustment really helped me to deal with my supposed weed problems. This was the hardest thing for me to understand. When a weed emerged in my garden, I wanted to remove it. Instead I learned the functions of these plants. They were often responding to a need in the soil. For example, clover provides nitrogen to infertile soils. Dandelions are great for loosening compacted soil with a strong tap root, and nutrient accumulators—like plantain and chicory—mine nutrients to the surface to be used by other plants.

The Author's Diverse Keyhole Garden

Understanding the uses and purposes of "weeds" helped me to see the beauty in a plant whose sole purpose is to make its home environment so fertile and complex that *it* is no longer needed. With this knowledge, and without the need for order and control, my weeding chores are a fraction of what they once were. A weed is any plant growing in a place where you do not want it. I have very few "weeds" because I am happy to coexist with plants that provide nitrogen fixation, nutrient accumulation, beneficial insect attraction, medicine, food, herbs, and diversity.

I am a big believer in building not just an orchard or a garden but an ecosystem. If you can build a varied and healthy ecosystem with tremendous diversity, Mother Nature will reward your efforts. And, if a plant fails or dies or succumbs to pests, it is nature's way of fixing a mistake in your design.

- The pesticide treadmill exists when applying pesticides upsets the natural balance of an ecosystem, thereby necessitating more pesticides.

- Healthy soil, better design, and a change of attitude is how I deal with weeds and insects without pesticides.

- A garden design that mimics nature is important for a successful pesticide-free garden.

- Understanding the uses and purposes of "weeds" helped me to see the beauty in a plant whose sole purpose is to make its home environment so fertile and complex that *it* is no longer needed.

In Chapter 8 the all-important element of clean drinking water is discussed.

8

WATER

While water is ubiquitous on our blue planet, freshwater is not. Only 2.5% of our planet's water is freshwater, the rest being salt water in our oceans. Of that 2.5%, 68.7% of the fresh-water is locked up in glaciers and ice caps, 30.1% in groundwater, and 1.2% in surface water such as permafrost, lakes, and rivers. Usable surface water is sliced even thinner when you consider that 69% of that 1.2% is locked up in ground ice and perma-frost. Lakes make up the largest slice of *usable* surface water,

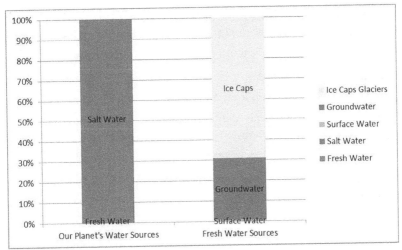

contributing 20.9%, but rivers are humans most often used source of water for much of the world, yet this source is only 0.49% of that 1.2% of existing fresh surface water.[26]

In the United States, over 50% of people obtain their water from groundwater.[27] Most rural Americans have wells with electric pumps to bring freshwater to their homes. Groundwater sources are more plentiful than surface water, but there is a price to pay to pull water from the ground. Without electricity, most of these rural homeowners are without water. Well pumps do break and need to be replaced, and water often needs to be treated. I have to fill up a water softener system with salt every few months, and I have an ultraviolet light to purify my water. Upon testing my water, I determined from my results that it was high in certain bacteria and pathogens, likely from manure runoff. This wasn't surprising given the amount of farms in the area.

A 2012 Chinese government study found 90% of their cities had contaminated groundwater.[28] I could not find one definitive *recent* study in regard to groundwater in the United States. I did find three studies performed by the USGS measuring various contaminants of groundwater. In 1992-2001 the USGS measured pesticide levels in shallow groundwater. They found one or more pesticides in enough concentration to cause a danger to human health in 4.8% of shallow groundwater in urban areas, 1.2% in

---

26 Peter H. Gleick, *Water in Crisis: A Guide to the World's Freshwater Resources* (Oxford, UK: Oxford University Press, 1993).

27 "What Is Groundwater?" *US Geological Survey* (January 1, 2014), http://pubs.usgs.gov/of/1993/ofr93-643/.

28 Jonathan Kaiman, "Chinese Environment Official Challenged to Swim in Polluted River," *Guardian News and Media United* (February 21, 2013), www.theguardian.com/environment/2013/feb/21/chinese-official-swim-polluted-river.

agricultural areas, and 1% in mixed-land uses.[29]

A USGS study conducted in 1997 tested groundwater contamination by nitrates (nitrogen fertilizers) and found much higher contamination percentages. In high-input areas, such as agricultural regions with well-drained soils and little forest, they found 24% of these wells below the drinking water standard.[30]

On the other end of the spectrum, in areas of low inputs, with poorly drained soils and lots of forest cover, they still found a 5% nitrate contamination. Most of the country was somewhere in between.[31] A more recent study conducted in 2009 examined the water quality of over 2000 private wells and determined 23% of these had at least one contaminant in enough concentration to present a health concern.[32]

Unfortunately, for much of the world's inhabitants who cannot afford wells and electricity, they are forced to rely on contaminated surface water. According to the EPA, 35% of rivers and streams and 45% of lakes in the United States are too polluted for fishing or even swimming.[33] In 2011 the Chinese government

29 Gilliom, R., P. Hamilton, "Pesticides in the Nation's Streams and Ground-water, 1992-2001: A Summary," *US Geological Survey* (March, 2006), http://pubs.usgs.gov/fs/2006/3028/.

30 Bernard Nolan, et al, "A National Look at Nitrate Contamination of Groundwater," *US Geological Survey* (August 31, 1997), http://water.usgs.gov/nawqa/nutrients/pubs/wcp_v39_no12/.

31 Ibid.

32 Jennifer LaVista, Leslie Desimone, "Contamination in US Private Wells," *US Geological Survey* (March 2009), http://water.usgs.gov/edu/gw-well-contamination.html.

33 "The Quality of Our Nation's Water," *Environmental Protection Agency* (1998),https://www.epa.gov/sites/production/files/2015-09/documents/1998_national_water_quality_inventory_report_to_congress.pdf.

reported that 43% of their state-monitored rivers were unsuitable for human contact. Up to 200 million rural Chinese have no access to clean drinking water.[34] Surface water tends to be more polluted than groundwater simply because of the filtering process that occurs above groundwater. This filtering phenomenon can be seen with deeper wells—usually cleaner than shallower wells. Surface water is much more prone to contaminant runoff.

According to UN-Water, water use has been growing at twice the rate of population growth. By 2025 an estimated 1.8 billion people will be living in countries or regions crippled by water scarcity, and two-thirds of the world's population will be living in water-stressed conditions.[35] This is an ecological disaster of epic proportions, one that will touch every human being on the face of this earth. Even if you live in a water-rich region, you may be affected by any one of the following: increased wars over water rights, refugees, higher costs of food, and polluted water.

As of April 7, 2015, 37% of the United States is in a state of at least moderate drought, with most of California in a state of severe drought.[36] Lake Mead—straddling the states of Nevada and Arizona—has endured a fourteen-year drought that has brought the lake which supplies Las Vegas to dangerously low

34 Jonathan Kaiman, "Chinese Environment Official Challenged to Swim in Polluted River," *Guardian News and Media United* (February 21, 2013), www.theguardian.com/environment/2013/feb/21/chinese-official-swim-polluted-river.

35 "UN Water factsheet on water security," *UN Water* (2006), www.un.org/waterforlifedecade/scarcity.shtml.

36 Mike Bostock, Kevin Quealy, "Mapping the Spread of Drought across the US," *The New York Times Company* (April 9, 2015), www.nytimes.com/interactive/2014/upshot/mapping-the-spread-of-drought-across-the-us.html?_r=0&abt=0002&abg=0.

levels. According to climate scientist Tim Barnett, by 2036, Lake Mead may no longer be able to provide any water to the City of Sin.[37]

Water scarcity isn't solely a West Coast issue. Georgia, Alabama, and Florida have been fighting over water rights since 1990. Georgia would like to continue to grow the Atlanta metro area, but overuse of Lake Lanier upstream from Alabama and Florida could cause problems for the downstream states.[38] If we already have states fighting among each other, it's not a stretch to imagine widespread water wars across the globe.

The Ogallala Aquifer that stretches 174,000 square miles across the Midwest from South Dakota to northwestern Texas is one of the biggest underground reservoirs of freshwater in the world. The breadbasket of the world depends on this resource. For decades farmers have been pumping more from the aquifer than it can refill itself. Since 1940, when irrigation began on the Great Plains, the water levels of the Ogallala are down at least 5 feet for much of the aquifer.[39]

For 20% of the Ogallala it is down 25 feet or more, and 11% has lost more than 50 feet. In some of the drought-stricken areas of Kansas and Texas, the aquifer is down more than 200 feet. The water pumped from the Ogallala Aquifer is much like what is seen in mining. It takes 6,000 years for water to percolate down into the reservoir for replenishment. If we pump it dry, with that

37 Emily Payne, "Is Sin City about to Run Dry?" *Associated Newspapers LTD* (July 1, 2014), www.dailymail.co.uk/travel/article-2676186/Is-Sin-City-run-dry-Las-Vegas-danger-running-water-14-year-drought.html.

38 "Tristate Water Dispute," *Wikipedia* (2014), http://En.wikipedia.org/wiki/Tri-state_water_dispute.

39 Jim Malewitz, "Ogallala Aquifer in Focus as Drought Ravages High Plains States," *HPMG News* (March 18, 2013), www.huffingtonpost.com/2013/03/18/ogallala-aquifer-drought_n_2902037.html.

6,000-year-replenishment time frame, it will essentially be gone forever.[40]

In my town we receive generous annual rainfall amounts of 45 inches or so, but we have storm-water runoff issues. I recently attended a municipal authority meeting in my community, where the board discussed storm water. They talked about the crumbling infrastructure of pipes and drains that would eventually need to be repaired or replaced. They were concerned about how they were going to pay for this. The consensus was that they would simply apply a tax to residents to begin building a fund.

One board member complained that Harrisburg and Lancaster were allowed to dump their waste directly into the river, but we had to make sure our storm water was clean. Another board member corrected him, saying that Harrisburg and Lancaster get fined for dumping. I wondered how you can put a price on clean water. The board was concerned about the storm-water permit for their MS-4—which stands for the municipal's separate storm sewer system.

The problem, according to the EPA, is that storm sewer systems commonly transport polluted water and dump them, untreated, directly into water bodies. The municipal authority must abide by the permit, which requires implementing at least six storm-water control measures, ranging from public education to elimination of illicit discharges.

I am familiar with storm-water runoff on my own property. When Denise and I first moved in, we had tremendous runoff down our hill that often ended up in the basements of my neighbors, downslope from us. One of my neighbors told me that I was ruining her life the first time I met her. She had considered legal action against me because of the runoff. Over the past five years, I've put in 2200 linear feet of swales, 4 ponds, 2000 trees,

40 Ibid.

Author's Site: Slowing Water with Ponds, Swales, and Trees

The Author's Fish Pond

and a 1000-gallon concrete cistern attached to my downspouts. Now rainfall is stored on and in my landscape, where it can be used by the plants. What once was six acres of heavy runoff will now hold the biggest rainfall events the region can deliver.

Water is a tricky thing. In some places, like Las Vegas, they don't have enough water, and, when they finally do get rain, it's usually a gully washer that becomes storm-water runoff. The Southwest and California are in terrible droughts, stressing already overburdened water sources, such as the Colorado River and Lake Mead. In other places, like the Midwest, they have issues with overpumping the Ogallala Aquifer and nitrogen contamination of their water. In my community, controlling storm-water runoff and dealing with contamination from farms is of paramount importance. Clean freshwater is becoming quite scarce.

These water problems didn't happen overnight. We've been on a slow-moving collision course with reality for quite some time. Typically, landscapers and homeowners alike do not place enough importance on water. Water conservation and use should be the first consideration in a landscape design. At my former company, clients who had areas that were too wet simply wanted to get rid of the water, and clients who had areas that were too dry would simply irrigate. Treating water as a nuisance or something to control leads to wasted water and additional storm-water runoff.

Water is a valuable resource to manage. A wet property might do well with natural ponds, wetlands, swales, and water-loving trees and plants to take advantage of the abundance. A dry property could also benefit from tree cover to reduce surface evaporation. Large swales are a great way for desert properties to hold onto those overdue large gully-washing rainstorms. Irrigation needs can be offset by heavy mulches or large water cisterns fed by downspouts to feed drip-irrigation systems. An inch of rain falling on a 1,000-square-foot roof will yield 623 gallons of water. We should endeavor to keep and use every drop of water that falls on our properties.

Swales, diversion drain, gray water, silt pond, and rooftop rainwater collection provides irrigation for garden and fresh water to fish pond. Fish pond overflows to swale downslope that irrigates fruit trees. Trees are white from kaolin clay.

In addition to wasting water, we pollute water resources with our pesticide use. Lawn treatment companies typically use liquid sprayers and large walk-behind rotary spreaders. These spreaders can hold one hundred pounds of granular material at a time and spread granules ten-feet-wide. They are tremendously efficient and durable. The problem they have is, when you need to apply a granular fertilizer and/or pesticide, it is impossible to apply to small areas without a lot of overspread.

The median strips in front of homes that lead directly into

the sewer system are a perfect example. These strips of grass are often only three feet wide. Even with a baffle attachment that can limit the fertilizer spread to six feet, it is impossible not to douse the sidewalk and curb with granular fertilizers and pesticides. My company did use the baffles on the spreaders to limit this problem.

We also blew the hard surfaces clean before finishing, but those granules in front of the curb near the street typically end up in the sewer, because it was difficult to blow the granules over the curb. Even homeowners who use smaller rotary spreaders typically have a six-foot-wide spread of granules. Most companies I came across did not use baffles, and tons of granules ended up in the street and along the curb. Some companies didn't even bother to blow the granules back into the lawn.

I know of quite a few companies that would spray an entire lawn with a mixture of fertilizer and herbicide, even if the lawn was weed-free, because that was the mix in their tanks that day. When using a liquid spray gun for a lawn, the technician walks back and forth, waving the gun quickly to spread the concoction evenly. It is easier to keep a liquid spray from ending up on the hard surfaces than granules that bounce and roll, but you cannot blow off a liquid spray, so it is inevitable that some pesticides and fertilizers will end up in the storm water runoff.

The UN estimates that desertification destroys approximately 29 million acres of land annually. This is land roughly equal to half the size of England.[41] The main culprit is the destruction of forests. Plants absorb more water than what they need because they lose water through evapotranspiration. This is how most air is humidified. Without evapotranspiration of plants, the interiors

41 Milton H. Saier Jr, "Desertification and Migration," *Water, Air, and Soil Pollution* (June 6, 2007), https://link.springer.com/article/10.1007/s11270-007-9429-6.

of continents would be deserts. Trees are by far the most effective plants at adding moisture to the air. An average tree contributes 250-400 gallons of water per day to the air through their leaves.[42]

When trees are cut from large expanses, this can slow or stop rain downwind. In our built landscapes and farms, trees should be the dominant feature. Instead grass and annual crops prevail, increasing erosion and desertification. By weight, topsoil is the biggest export of the United States. Through erosion, we send one of our most valuable resources down our rivers, into the ocean, further polluting our waterways in the process.

The sad part of this story is that this monumental calamity is preventable. Imagine if, instead of paying for pesticides and fertilizers to be dumped on your grass and into your water, you used that money to plant trees. Imagine if landscapers designed their projects to use water as the life-giving resource that it is, not a nuisance to get rid of. The more trees we plant and water we store in the landscape, the easier it becomes to grow more trees, rehydrate the land, and heal the hydrologic cycle.

- Only 2.5% of our planet's water is freshwater.

- By 2025 an estimated 1.8 billion people will be living in countries or regions crippled by water scarcity, and two-thirds of the world's population will be living in water-stressed conditions.

- As of April 7, 2015, 37% of the United States is in a state of at least moderate drought, with most of California in a state of severe drought.

- Water wars are likely to spread across the globe.

---

42 Jack Rowe, "Trees and the Water Cycle," *Permaculture and Sanity* (n.d.), http://permaculture-and-sanity.com/pcarticles/trees-and-the-water-cycle.php.

- Our nation's biggest aquifer, the Ogallala that supplies Midwestern farmers, is being pumped unsustainably.

- In addition to wasting water, we pollute our water resources with pesticides.

- Desertification and drought destroys approximately 29 million acres annually. This is land roughly equal to half the size of England.

- Water can and should be stored in the landscape, where it can grow trees, repair the hydrologic cycle, be used by the occupants, and prevented from contributing to the pollution caused by storm-water runoff.

The next chapter explains why you should fire your landscaper.

9

FIRE THE LANDSCAPER

As a landscape company owner, I had the theory that we should be a one-stop shop. Clients should be able to acquire every outdoor service from us. I thought our services would be synergistic. If someone signed up for a large design/build project, we could also handle the maintenance after the installation. The quality of our workmanship and the wide breadth of services we offered made my business one of the fastest growing landscape companies in the suburbs of Washington, DC. In eight years we went from gross revenues of less than $10,000 to over $5 million. We were one of the few companies that could offer a wide variety of services.

Many others were very specialized. For example, TruGreen, Lawn Doctor, Scotts, and Natural Lawn all specialized in lawn treatments. Still others only offer design/build or lawn maintenance, like mowing and weeding. For this chapter I would like to talk about the companies involved in design/build or landscaping and why you should fire your landscaper.

In order to explain the landscape industry in a way that makes sense, let's pretend you are going to hire a company to design and install a landscape for your new home. It's early spring, and you're excited to get going! The first thing you do is go online and find all the companies that service your area. Chances are, if you have any population density at all, there'll be countless companies to choose from.

If you're reading this book, maybe you care about the environment and want to find a "green" landscaper or one who claims with great pride that they are in fact "going green!" First, let me say that I detest it when people and companies say they're "going green." Mostly, it's just marketing for companies and fashion for individuals.

My former company has a nice little piece on their website about how they're "going green and staying that way!" I read through the marketing, and I'm sure it's all true, but these are all things they would do anyway. These things make marketing sense from a business standpoint. It's another way to sell you more stuff that you don't need. If the landscape industry really cared about Mother Nature, they'd stop designing and installing landscapes that look and function nothing like nature.

Despite my advice about the "going green" nonsense, you go ahead and contact five companies that claim to be "green" and request an estimate. You're surprised that only two of them answer the phone with a live person, forcing you to leave a message for the other three. Of the two who answer the phone, one requires a fee of fifty dollars to schedule an appointment to meet with a landscape designer. They say, if you hire them, you will get the fifty dollars credited to your account. I know what you're thinking: fifty bucks just to come out is a rip-off.

At my former company, we used to do "free" landscape design consultations. We wasted time on "tire kickers" who were only interested in free advice or price shopping. I remember doing a design for one of these "tire kickers." I used my turf-marking paint to show the guy where I'd put the plants. I left him a contract, but I never heard from him. I drove by his house a few weeks later, and there was my design already done.

When my company started charging for consultations, this eliminated the "tire kickers" and freed up more time to spend with qualified clients. Our clients ended up with better designs because we weren't wasting valuable time in the spring chasing poor leads. With consultations and designs, you typically get what you pay for. The companies that charge to send designers to meet with you do so because they are good enough to command a fee.

For the purpose of this story, we'll call the company with the initial fee "Gettin' Paid Landscaping." You agree to the fifty-dollar fee, and you schedule an appointment. You also schedule an appointment with the "free consult" company, which we'll call "Budget Landscape." Only one of the three other companies that you left messages for calls you back. You schedule an appointment with that company as well, which we'll call "Going Green Landscaping."

All three companies tell you that the first opening for an appointment they have is early May, which is two weeks away. You're disappointed with the wait, but you acquiesce and schedule the appointments all for the same day, one in the morning, one at lunchtime, and one in the afternoon.

The appointment day finally comes. You meet with Gettin' Paid Landscaping in the morning, and they impress you with their flashy business cards and extensive portfolio of work they've done around town. The designer brags that he has a degree in landscape architecture, which impresses you. As an aside, I have worked with designers with degrees in landscape architecture and those without any degree whatsoever. The best designer I have ever worked with, bar none, has no degree. Okay, back to the story.

You walk around your property with the landscape architect, talking about options and possibilities for your landscape. He takes notes, asks questions, and offers a few suggestions, intently gauging your response. After an hour of walking and talking, he takes ten minutes to write up a contract to do a design for $500. This fee is for the plans only, not for the labor and materials to implement the design.

"Do you need to come back for more information for the design?" you ask.

"I just need to take a few measurements," he replies.

"How do you come up with your designs? Do you have a system?"

He stares at you blankly, as if he's never thought of that before. "I guess my system is what we just did. I walk the property with the client and take measurements and notes."

You were hoping for something a bit more elaborate.

He rushes off to his next appointment, leaving you with the contract.

At lunch you meet with Budget Landscape. The young designer seems hurried and stressed. He takes down your requests like a waiter at TGI Friday's.

"I think a low hedge along your bay window in front would be nice," he says. "Maybe hollies or boxwoods, and skinny evergreens to frame the house at the corners. Maybe junipers pruned in a spiral shape. We could do some low-maintenance perennials in front of the hedge."

You nod.

"We'll make the bed lines curvy. Long, large curves look more natural than straight lines."

You nod.

"A rock retaining wall on the corner of the house, where there's a slope, would be nice. You could also use a patio in back, with some plantings to provide privacy."

His suggestions make sense to you, but they seem very similar to what everyone in your suburban neighborhood already has. Before he leaves, he writes up a contract for the design in the amount of $300.

In the afternoon you meet with Going Green Landscaping. The designer is friendly and confident. She walks the property with you like the previous designers.

"I'd love to do a foundation hedge in front of the bay window," she says. "Azaleas or rhododendrons would be nice to give you some color."

You nod.

These plants don't do well pruned as formal hedges, but you don't know that.

"I think we should put in a rock wall at the corner of the house and a patio in back. I'd love to add a few large trees to break up the large expanse of grass."

You nod.

"Are you interested in a sprinkler system? It's a pain to drag hoses around to water the plantings."

You nod. "Sounds like a good idea."

She tells you that she'll get back to you with a design and a contract for the job. She never mentions a price for the design.

My biggest criticism of landscape designers is that they have no system for designing a property. They do walk the property and talk to the client, and they might even take some notes, but in general they come up with their designs purely based on experience, what looks good, what the local nursery has, and what the client wants.

A good designer will figure out the sunny and shady areas of your property. I use a handy tool called a solar pathfinder to tell me exactly how much sun and shade a particular area has

Suburban Food Desert

for every time of the year. This will help to put the right plants in the right place. I try to determine prevailing wind directions. I can usually figure this out by looking at the trees, talking to the client, and using a simple flag on a post. This will help with establishing windbreaks where needed.

I dig in a few different areas on the property to determine soil types. I observe wet and dry areas. If the client doesn't have a good contour map, I will use a laser level to make one. This will help with placements of swales, ponds, diversion drains, pathways, and fences. The most important thing that needs to be done is to simply take the time to observe the site.

Before I even begin the design, I will make seven maps: a sun-and-shade map, a wind map, a soil map, a contour map, a moisture map, a map of the current features, and an observation map. Really good designing takes quite a bit longer than your landscaper is willing to spend on your property and might cost four to five times what your landscaper is charging.

The benefit of all this is a design that will be more natural, productive, beautiful, lower maintenance, sustainable and that will create a healthy ecosystem for the long term. Good design won't need replacement in ten years. Good design won't require pesticides. Good design plans for succession. Good design meets the needs of the inhabitants.

Another three weeks go by, and you finally get the contracts and designs back from your three designers. It is now June, and it's getting warm. The spring planting season is waning. Two of the designs are displayed from computer-derived maps. The free design is hand-drawn. All three of the designs feature purely ornamental plantings. There are no intentionally edible plantings suggested. The plans feature plants commonly found at your local nursery.

Water is only planned for with mechanical irrigation systems. There are no swales, gravity irrigation, rainwater catchment tanks, net-and-pan drainage, or natural ponds. The three plans are different in that one is more formal than the next or has different plant varieties, but, in general, the designs are very similar. They all feature a rock wall on the corner of the house and foundation plantings in a front bed of mulch with long sweeping curvaceous bed lines. They all have a patio in back with plantings around it and mulch as the ground cover. The designers talk lovingly about how great it will look! The truth of the matter is that the designers are all selling slightly different versions of the same poor landscape. It shouldn't be surprising to you. We learned about our obsession with conformity in Chapter 5.

The plant selections of our esteemed landscape designers are typically based on what they know and what they can easily obtain. Most landscapers buy from their local nursery at a discount or from a wholesale nursery at a much deeper discount. If they sell plants available from the wholesale nursery, their profit on the plant material is typically higher because the plants are cheaper. With their bulk discounts on common plants, they can often mark up your plant material 100%. The problem with that is the quality is often lower and the selection is not as varied.

Take a walk around your neighborhood and observe the similarity among the types of plants. Then take a trip to the nursery to see the same plants. The landscapers and nurserymen will tell you that the plants they install are low maintenance. I will agree that the plants they install are typically foolproof low-maintenance plantings that don't die right away. These are the perfect plants to cover up poor designs where zero thought is placed into creating a functioning, interconnected ecosystem. These plants are suitable for existing in an unnatural environment without complaint.

On my six-acre property, I have planted over 2000 trees and shrubs. Approximately 90% of these plants cannot be found at my local nursery and certainly not at a wholesale nursery. The plants I have chosen for my property *are* beautiful, but they were chosen for their multifunctionality. Many of these plants are edible or medicinal herbs, and/or provide edible fruits or nuts. Many provide animal habitat, beneficial insect habitat through the nectar of their flowers, nitrogen fixation, nutrient accumulation, and pollinator attraction. The plants in much of suburbia exist on a mulch island solely to look pretty. They exist in a stasis of artificiality, where nothing grows, nothing dies, and everything looks tidy.

Before the supermarket and suburbia, people saw the wisdom in planting edibles at their homes. Most had small orchards and gardens. People foraged for wild edibles. They hunted; they gardened, and they dried and canned their harvests. Of late there has been a renaissance of sorts in edible landscaping with the local and sustainable food movements. Despite those efforts, the vast majority of suburbia and our cities are food deserts. If it weren't for the eighteen-wheelers delivering food to supermarkets, these people would starve.

The rural areas of our country are only slightly better with the farms poisoned by pesticides, and most of the produce in the form of corn and soy is for animal consumption. As I write this in early November 2014, I can hear the five-hundred-thousand-dollar John Deere harvester working my neighbor's field. It makes me sick to think of all the useless plant material being installed daily in these food deserts, when fruits, vegetables, and herbs could have easily been substituted. A design that doesn't provide at least a portion of a family's needs is a poor design. In eleven years as the majority owner of a large landscaping company, I *never* saw one design at my company or anyone else's that tried to do this.

This begs the question: why don't designers incorporate edibles into their designs? Some of this goes back to Chapter 5, where it's simply hard to deviate from the herd. Some of this has to do with plant availability and the inertia of the status quo. In fairness, I am starting to see a few landscape companies offering edible landscaping, which is a response to the recent popularity of healthy local food.

A few years ago, I had a conversation with my ex-business partner, who is now the sole owner of my former company. I suggested that he incorporate edibles into his clients' designs. He proceeded to tell me how his clients would hate the mess that dropping fruit would cause. That comment made me think about the design consultations that I've been on. The majority of these clients who I met with looked to *me* to tell them what to do. I was the "expert." They didn't know or could care less.

I could've peppered the northern Virginia suburbs with beautiful edible plants. I think my clients would've loved it! With the volume of clients my company had consulted, we could've started an edible plant revolution in the suburbs. Unfortunately, I missed that opportunity out of ignorance.

All right, sorry for the tangent; let's go back to the story. You have the three designs in hand, and you pick the most expensive one, from Gettin' Paid Landscaping. You reason, they all seem similar, but the expensive one has to be better somehow. You've waited a month and a half from the day you first called just to get the design, so you're anxious to get your project started before the spring planting season is over. After you've paid the initial deposit of $7,000, the designer informs you that they have a monthlong backlog, so they won't install your project until mid-July.

You cringe, then blurt out, "But that's why I called you in April."

"I'm sorry, there's nothing I can do about it," the designer replies.

"Won't it be too hot to plant in mid-July?"

"The plants will be fine. You just have to keep them watered. If any do die, they're covered under our plant warranty."

One of the biggest obstacles a landscape company has to overcome is the seasonality of their business. Spring is crazy busy, then the summer is slow. It picks up again in the fall, then the winter is completely dead. To install the most landscapes they can, they have to extend plantings into the summer. Yes, it's too hot and dry to be planting in the summer, but they do it anyway, reasoning the client can water, and, if plants die, they have a warranty from the nursery. Often most of the plants do live, but they are stunted by being planted with poor timing.

Your install date finally arrives the week after the July 4th weekend. Your landscaper was too busy trying to get projects done before the big holiday weekend to get to yours. They roll up to your house at 8:00 a.m. on Monday in their Ford F-450, pulling a dump trailer. Their employees are polite and dressed in uniforms clearly marked with the company logo. They work quickly and efficiently.

They build the patio and stonewall first. It takes four days to complete. On the final day of the week they install the planting beds; they plant over a hundred potted plants and install the mulch for a clean look. You are shocked that they were able to complete your project so quickly. You do a little math and figure out that you paid about $60 per man-hour or $180 per hour for three men to have the work done. You are left with a well-ordered landscape that is very much like your neighbor's.

Potted plants are the absolute worst way to establish plants. Landscapers use potted plants almost exclusively. I have never seen a landscaper use a bare-root or a direct-seeded tree or shrub. As I mentioned before, I have planted over 2000 trees and shrubs here on my property in various forms. I have planted many potted plants here, as well as bare-root and direct-seeded plants. Potted plants are by far the most expensive and most laborious way to plant trees and shrubs. They are also the form most likely to die or simply underperform.

Bare-root trees and shrubs can be ordered online and planted in the early spring before the buds break. These plants are much cheaper, and the selection is near infinite. Bare-root plants are just as they sound. They are trees and shrubs that will arrive without leaves and without soil attached to their roots. This makes them incredibly light and easy to ship. I have had much better results with these trees thriving over my transplants that originated in pots. The negative to be considered is the short planting window.

The best way to establish trees and shrubs is directly seeded.

Trees and shrubs established this way never face transplant shock. They will grow more vigorous and pest resistant than their bare-root or potted counterparts. Seed is also much cheaper than the transplants, and the labor to install seed is miniscule. The exciting thing about seed is you can plant ten seeds in an area where you would like one tree, then, over time, remove the less dominant trees, thereby genetically selecting the healthiest trees.

Let's revisit our fictitious landscape project. Your landscape installation was completed in the middle of July. After two months of brutal heat, half of your plants die. You call your designer.

"Have you been watering?" he asks. "This summer's been so hot."

"I've been dragging hoses around all summer," you respond through gritted teeth.

"You should've purchased that irrigation system I recommended."

You bite your tongue.

"Don't worry, we'll replace anything that's dead. Wait until next spring and we'll see what leafs out."

The following spring rolls around, and your plants are still dead. You call back the designer, and he says he'll take a look at the plants and get them replaced. You relax a bit, knowing that the company will honor their warranty.

You think, *this is why I paid $14,000 to a professional company.*

Two weeks pass, and your plants haven't been replaced, and you haven't heard from anyone. You call the designer again.

"I meant to call you," he says. "My boss said we can't honor the warranty because the plants weren't watered enough. I'm sorry, but the warranty doesn't cover drought. He did offer to replace the plants for our cost, which is about half of what you paid. And we won't charge any labor because we take good care of our clients."

- Going green is all about marketing.

- Landscape designers have no system for designing a property.

- Good design won't need replacement or require pesticides, but does plan for succession, and meets the needs of the inhabitants.

- Most landscape designs are similar, firmly entrenched among the status quo.

- Potted plants are the most labor intensive and expensive types of plants.

- Bare-root or direct-seeded trees and shrubs yield better plants at a fraction of the price.

In the next chapter, we move on to firing whoever mows your lawn.

10

FIRE THE LAWN MOWING COMPANY (YES, THE NEIGHBOR'S KID TOO)

The first service I ever offered in the landscape industry was mowing. It's a simple service with a low barrier to entry. Anyone with a pickup truck and a mower can start a company. If you have a mowing service, you should fire them. You might have a young kid who mows your lawn, not a professional company. If so, you should probably fire the little punk too.

The number one reason is something we've already touched on in this book. They mow entirely too often. Running a seven-hundred-pound machine back and forth on your property every week damages soil life, stifles diversity, and encourages compaction-fighting "weeds." To add insult to injury, lawn services push expensive aeration jobs to fight the compaction they've caused and then herbicides to kill weeds that are simply trying to fix the damage to the soil.

Even if you don't apply herbicides and allow Mother Nature to grace you with her diversity of plant species, constantly mowing these plants down to an inch of their life will negate many of the benefits of a meadow. The plants won't have a chance to flower, reproduce, and provide pollen and nectar to beneficial insects and pollinators. The shorter you keep your lawn, the shorter the root system of the plants contained therein. Closely mown plants are more prone to drought, disease, and insect damage.

I realize that most people would get in quite a bit of trouble with lawns that are four feet tall, but, if you aren't pumping up the lawn with chemical fertilizers and wasting water to keep it growing, then you could reduce your mowing frequency dramatically. You might have to mow every two weeks in the spring to keep up with the lush growth, but you could reduce your frequency to once a month for much of the season. You'd also need to raise your mowing height as tall as possible, which is usually four inches or so.

Many of the beneficial meadow plants don't tolerate constant close mowing like grass, so the higher cut will help establish plants like clover, alfalfa, yarrow, wild carrot, and chicory. This would allow for your meadow to grow, flower, and thrive. Your property would be an oasis for bees and beneficial insects in a sea of poison and closely cropped monoculture wastelands.

If you have a lawn service that would agree to mow every two weeks in the spring, back off to once a month after that, plus mow at a height of four inches, then I'd keep them on. That's a tall order for most companies which mow weekly, and, even if they agreed to the infrequent schedule, they may not be able to accommodate the increased mowing height. Some commercial mowers do not have easily adjustable blade heights. It often requires the removal of the blades, and then spacers rearranged.

Mowing services and design/build companies have similar headaches with scheduling. The grass grows twice as fast in the spring as it does any other time of the year. It is very difficult for companies to keep up. My lawn-mowing crews often had to mow the lawns twice in the spring to eliminate the clumps of lush grass that had been cut and then strewn about the yard. We would spend 25-50% longer servicing a property in the spring than we would in the heat of the summer, when the growth was sparse. Coupled with the abundance of spring rainouts, we were often scrambling to keep up.

Summertime was a different story. We'd finish our routes early, often mowing properties that didn't really need to be mowed. We used to joke that we were "striping up the dirt." This is why many companies have a hard time keeping your lawn cut in the spring when it needs it, but they are all over it in the summer when it's less necessary. This phenomenon is for cool-season grass in temperate climates. For those of you living in the South with warm-season grass, like zoysiagrass or Bermuda grass, the growing season is during the warm and wet times of the year.

Many mowing services will also offer weeding services for your driveway, sidewalks, and planting beds. This usually consists of walking around with a sprayer filled with herbicide to eliminate anything green in the sea of brown mulch, black asphalt, and gray concrete. This never-ending cycle of nature trying to fix the deficiencies in your soil, while the lawn technician kills the "weeds," only serves to pollute your property and keep your soil in a constant state of infancy.

I've seen plenty of incompetent technicians accidentally kill garden seedlings with herbicide. I remember one particularly egregious company that dumped gasoline on the weeds growing in the concrete. The lawn tech said that gasoline stops anything from growing there for years!

- Lawns are mowed too often, damaging soil life, stifling diversity, and increasing compaction.

- Most beneficial meadow plants do not tolerate close mowing.

Now that we've discussed not hiring companies to thwart Mother Nature, in the next chapter we'll talk about avoiding companies that poison properties with pesticides.

11

STOP POISONING YOUR PROPERTY

How would you like it if I sprayed a poison on your property, killing edible and beneficial plants, and destroying soil life? Then I had the audacity to demand payment. It's insane that people pay to have their properties poisoned. The plethora of lawn care companies offering treatments for your lawn and plants should absolutely be fired.

Adding a fertilizer to your lawn or plants isn't necessarily a bad thing. I add fertilizer in the form of organic material and compost to my garden, and the soil life thanks me by growing beautiful, healthy fruits, herbs, flowers, and vegetables. The problem with the fertilizers that commercial companies typically apply is that they are synthetic chemical fertilizers. These chemical fertilizers contain salts that are absorbed rapidly by the plants. This is why plants grow quickly after an application. The problem is that the plants are fed, but the soil life is not.

The salts can repel beneficial soil life, like earthworms, by acidifying the soil. With a decline in the soil life, the soil structure and water-holding capabilities decline. This decline causes increased leeching of the fertilizers, turning your plants into addicts, needing more and more fertilizer for the same effect.

Meanwhile, the soil life is dead, and those fertilizers end up adding to the pollution of our drinking water, streams, rivers, and finally our oceans.

Some companies offer organic fertilizers but beware, as it is usually only a part of their fertilizer mixture. When I ran the fertilizer program at my former company, we did use organic fertilizers, but it wasn't for every treatment. Our organic fertilizer of choice was Milorganite, which is derived from activated human sewage sludge, otherwise known as human feces. I know it sounds awful, but organic fertilizers are much safer and better for the environment than chemical fertilizers. Or at least that's what we thought.

The Environmental Protection Agency and others have shown that biosolids can contain measurable levels of heavy metals, contaminants from pharmaceuticals, personal care products, steroids, and hormones. In 2007, toxic PCBs (polychlorinated biphenyl) were detected in Milorganite.[43] I don't know if my old company still uses the product, but I can say that we used the product with the best of intentions, and notwithstanding the contaminants found in Milorganite, typically organic fertilizers are better for plants and the environment than chemical fertilizers.

Plenty of companies offer treatments that claim to be environmentally friendly. Like our "green" landscapers mentioned earlier, beware of the marketing. Some companies claim that they are better for the environment because they use granular applications instead of sprays. Meanwhile those granular chemical fertilizers contain the salts referenced above.

Almost every company that I came into contact with, in my eleven years in landscaping, used fertilizers laced with

43 "Milorganite," *Wikipedia* (2018), https://en.wikipedia.org/wiki/Milorganite.

preemergent herbicide in the early spring. This chemical fertilizer is coated with an herbicide that stops annual weeds from germinating. It is applied at a high-enough rate to keep weeds—like crabgrass, goosegrass, barley, oats, ryegrass, spurge, chickweed, henbit, mustard, oxalis, bitter cress, and many others—from germinating for up to six months.

Many of these so-called weeds are excellent herbs. Oxalis has a great lemony flavor that I like to add to salads. Chickweed and henbit provide valuable winter ground covers that my chickens love to eat. Unless your treatment company tries to educate you on the benefits of cultivating common "weeds," they are not environmentally friendly.

In my opinion, lawn and plant treatment services are the most unethical part of the landscape industry. I find it interesting that it is also the most lucrative. In terms of dollars per man-hour, our treatment program was by far the most profitable service we offered. It was routine for a single technician to bring in $1,000 in one day. After you factor out the material cost of the product, he was bringing into the company about $75-$85 per man-hour. A mowing or landscape crew typically earned $45-$65 per man-hour. Even with the high profit margins, I saw some very questionable business practices among our competitors. I was friendly with a manager of one of the large companies in this field. He told me that they had a problem with "ghosting" lawns.

I asked, "What the hell is 'ghosting'?"

He proceeded to tell me, if it looked like nobody was home, guys would simply put the notice on the door as if they had done the treatment. As good as my company was, we were not immune to this form of theft. Many years ago, I was reviewing a route from one of our technicians, and the time allotted did not seem realistic for the amount of work completed. I went out to the properties, which were mostly townhomes, to check the work. We were applying a granular fertilizer, so I could see the granules on the ground, if the work had been done.

I went from house to house, and everything looked fine, but something nagged me. I didn't feel like walking all the way around the row of houses to check the backyards. Then it occurred to me that maybe the technician didn't feel like walking around either. I checked the backyards, and, bingo, I found the pattern. He simply skipped all the backyards. I fired him the next day, and we went back and finished the work.

Another inherent disadvantage to using these chemical fertilizers and pesticides is that, if they are applied in the wrong conditions, they can burn the foliage of the plants, whether it's a lawn or a hedgerow. I've seen quite a few torched lawns in my day, mostly by a couple of the big companies in this field. Again, my former company wasn't immune here either.

I remember accidentally dumping my spreader on a lawn that had a severe slope. I tried to clean it up, but, less than a week later, the area was burnt. I repaired it with sod, free of charge. I remember a mishap where one of our technicians sprayed horticultural oil on a blue juniper. The oil removed the bluish color from the side of the tree that was accidentally sprayed, so half the tree was green, and half was blue. We had another technician who was fired for applying treatments to the wrong houses. This got us in trouble with the state, when he applied chemicals to a person's lawn who said she had terrible allergies to the sprays.

These lawn care companies, like the mowing services and landscapers of the previous chapters, have similar scheduling and timing issues. "Weeds" come quick in the spring, and herbicides are only effective over 55 degrees. Yet when temperatures exceed 85 degrees and include dry conditions, these factors can lead to chemical burn of turf grasses. Herbicides are also ineffective if it rains within a few hours of the application.

Grub-control treatments applied too late in the summer are ineffective against mature grubs. Seed simply broadcast over the grass doesn't germinate without seed-soil contact. Seed applied too late in the fall has reduced germination. The challenge for these companies is to jam-pack as many clients as possible into their routes, which leads to many applications being done with poor timing.

As a former consultant to the landscape industry, I encouraged my clients to give their customers a chemical-free option filled with appropriately timed organic fertilizers, compost additions, and compost tea sprays, coupled with a healthy dose of ecological education. Clients can have healthier, more beautiful, lower-maintenance ecosystems without chemicals, if we can just let go of our obsession with neatness and conformity.

- Most lawn care companies apply synthetic fertilizers that contain salts which are harmful to beneficial soil life.

- In my opinion the lawn and plant treatment services are the most unethical part of the landscape industry.

- Chemical-free options do exist.

If you live in a residential area governed by an HOA, the next chapter is for you.

12

KILL THE HOA

As a conventional landscaper, the HOA was a boon to my business. Many homeowners associations force residents to maintain their properties in a neatly kept "weed"-free condition. This pushes many people to hire a landscaper to keep them from getting in trouble with neighbors or their HOA. My company was hired many times to clean up properties that had not been mowed or weeded.

In these instances the HOAs were not concerned about price. They were concerned about how quickly we could do the work. Pricing here wasn't a worry for the HOA because these services were being billed to the homeowner directly. Of course, when it came to the maintenance of the common grounds, the HOA always procured multiple competitive bids. Back then I never thought about what the homeowner had to go through because his or her property was not up to the HOA's standards.

For a populace that talks tough about freedom and liberty, we sure love to limit the freedom and liberty of others. Home-owners associations across the country have done an excellent job violating basic human rights and mandating the continued destruction of our ecosystems.

*Suburban Neighborhood: Wide Expanse of Asphalt
and Chemically Treated and Closely Cropped Grass*

Wessex is an upscale (their word, not mine) community in Cary, North Carolina, with 202 homes with price tags ranging from $500,000 to over $1 million. Located near Raleigh and Chapel Hill, the community boasts that you can live in a dream home, with the convenience of shopping and recreation, without sacrificing the "serenity and peace of a quiet neighborhood." I bet it's not so serene and peaceful if you violate the long list of rules the HOA forces on its residents. This excerpt (spelling and grammar left as is) comes from page 1 of the Wessex HOA Lawn and Garden Maintenance Guidelines:

> Your home must meet the standards established by our Covenants: a well-tended lawn and planting beds. You MUST use some sort of weed-feed & pre-emergent weed

control on your lawn twice each year. If you do not, your lawn will be mostly weeds. You will receive a letter from our management company stating your lawn does not meet standards. It will take significant work and funds to bring it up to an appropriate level and you may risk fines. The cost to comply will be more than the amount you would spend over five years by following the recommended guidelines.[44]

Here we have an HOA forcing its residents to use chemicals on their properties. I can't imagine paying one million dollars for a home, then being forced to poison it.

What a marketing pitch: "You've just purchased your dream home for 1.1 million dollars. Guess what you've won! That's right, a higher risk of cancer and autism for your family, especially if you have young children!"

The Wessex HOA isn't unique in requiring residents to use chemicals. I found many homeowners associations with similar requirements. Even the ones that don't specifically require chemicals do require "weed"-free landscapes. This "weed"-free look requires chemicals to do this efficiently. In Atlanta, Georgia, the Willbrooke Homeowner's Association Yard Care Rules and Regulations on page 1 cites the following (again, no changes were made to correct its spelling and grammar errors):

Lawn maintenance is a year-round requirement with some seasons requiring more attention than others. Regardless of the season, a neat appearance must be maintained. Weeds sprouting up in the lawn or, weeds that are allowed

44 Wessex HOA, "Wessex HOA Lawn and Garden Maintenance Guidelines," (n.d.), www.wessexhoa.org/pdfs/Wessex_HOA_Annual_Lawn_and_Garden_Maintenance_Guidelines.pdf.

to dominate the make-up of the "lawn", must be eliminated by hand or by chemical means. The landscaping must be maintained on every Lot consistent with the Community-Wide Standard (e.g., foundation plantings, lawn areas). Weeding, mulching, edging, fertilization, and insect control of the lawn and all plantings is also required.[45]

In summary, Willbrooke requires a "neat" appearance that you can achieve through hand-weeding or through an herbicide. Hand-weeding a lawn is a tedious, time-consuming job that never ends. Remember our chapter on succession. Mother Nature will keep sending those weeds to fix the problems in your soil. This community also requires fertilization and insect control. I wonder how they enforce that requirement.

I suppose if the lawn isn't green enough, they could cite the homeowner with not fertilizing, or, if they have visible grub damage, they could cite them for not applying an insecticide. That could get tricky because a fertilized lawn is not a guarantee of a green lawn, and applying insecticides does not guarantee no insect damage. Continued use of insecticides over time breeds resistant pests and destroys beneficial insects. Continued use of chemical fertilizers adds salt to the soil, destroying soil life. This is the concept of the pesticide treadmill we learned about in Chapter 7.

I found Willbrooke's requirement to maintain the landscaping "consistent with the Community-Wide Standard (e.g., foundation plantings, lawn areas)" particularly appalling. This further supports my assertion that, through culture and legislation, our landscapes have become homogenous, monotonous, and unproductive. To drive the final nail in the coffin of productive

45 Willbrooke HOA, "Yard Care Rules and Regulations," (n.d.), www.willbrooke.org/covenants/Yardcarerequirementsfinalrevised.pdf.

landscapes, Willbrooke makes it difficult for anyone to garden, per Willbrooke Homeowner's Association Yard Care Rules and Regulations, with the following rules, on pages 2 and 3.

> All **vegetable gardens** must be located out of view from the street with proper screening and/or integration with a general landscape plan. All vegetable plants must be included in a landscape plan approved in advance by **ARC** (Architectural Review Committee).

> **Fruit trees** must be cared for to prevent noxious insect infestation.

> No changes or barriers in the **original flow of drainage** water in the Community shall be made.

> No **compost areas or containers** for any location on any Lot have been approved by **ARC**.[46]

I have a ten-thousand-square-foot vegetable garden, bigger than most suburban lawns, prominently displayed in my front yard. I love my garden; it provides the healthiest, best-tasting produce I've ever had. I strategically placed it in front of my home because that's where the sun is, and it's easily accessible. It's also beautiful, with flowers, "weeds," vegetables, fruit trees, kiwi and grapevines, berries, and a flock of chickens coexisting in an oasis of abundance. I can't imagine having to hide my garden, as if it were something to be ashamed of or something ugly.

The Willbrooke HOA in Georgia should be ashamed of the community life they've forced on their residents. As an ecological designer, I know that the most important part of any landscape is

46 Ibid, 2, 3.

water. Since 1999 Georgia has been in drought more often than not.[47] By mandating a high-maintenance water-intensive landscape and not allowing changes to the flow of drainage water, they—and other HOAs like them—are a big part of the dwindling-freshwater-supply problem. Slowing down the flow of water runoff by creating barriers is an excellent way to conserve and reuse water. I use swales, ponds, diversion drains, berms, trees, and heavy mulches to passively store rainwater in the landscape of my residence. This creates a drought-proof environment that helps to recharge local aquifers.

By banning compost bins, the Willbrooke HOA makes damn sure that all your "trash," whether it is organic material or not, must end up in a landfill. The best garden composts are often made from what people are forced to put into trash bags. Food scraps, leaves, and unsprayed grass clippings make terrific compost ingredients.

The Master Homeowners Association for Green Valley Ranch in Colorado is another place where the environment is being abused. Per the Green Valley Ranch Homeowner's Association Landscape Violation Frequently Asked Questions page 2, below are their definitions of landscape violations (with misspellings and grammar errors left as is):

> **Weeds/grass in rocks/mulch** - This means you have a rock or mulch area that has weeds or grass in it. This area needs to be weed AND grass free. Simply put - look at your rock or mulch beds. Any plant material that was not intentionally planted (bushes, flowers) should not be there. The weeds need to be removed; simply spraying them will not

47 Neela Banerjee, "Georgia Officials Give Drought the Silent Treatment," *Los Angeles Times* (September 16, 2012), http://articles.latimes.com/2012/sep/16/nation/la-na-georgia-drought-20120916.

cure the violation as dead weeds still present still represent a violation.

Bare spots in the lawn - This is an area, large or small, in your lawn that does not have grass. These are caused by several issues, including dog urine, not enough moisture, fungus or bugs (pests) in the grass. Any bare spots in the grass need to be repaired, either by seed or sod. Finding out the cause of the spots is a vital first step, so you know how to treat the area and prevent having to fix this problem time and time again.

Tree-like Shape - Trees must be pruned regularly, including cutting any "sucker" branches on the bottom and making sure the leaves are in a generally rounded "tree-like" shape. Basically, the trees need to look like a traditional tree.

Weeds in the grass - Any areas in the yard that have grass need to have only grass; no weeds are permitted. This includes obvious weeds such as dandelions and thistles, but also includes less obvious weeds, such as crab grass, etc.

Dry Areas of Lawn - This is an area of the lawn that has grass, but it is dry. In a lot of cases, simply increasing watering should help. Sometimes using a product like Revive that helps with water absorption can also help with dry grass. This area of town is famous for our sandy soil base which has a poor water absorption for grass roots. Using an annual protocol of aeration and top dressing with a quality compost significantly helps with using less water and achieving healthy green grass.

Sparse areas of Lawn - In order to be in compliance, the grass in your lawn must be healthy, and grass must fill in the entire area that is designated to be grass. You will get a letter if your grass does not do this.[48]

These guys really hate weeds! Even if you kill every "weed" on your property, it's still not good enough. You also have to dispose of the weed carcasses. I'm guessing you take those unpleasant dead plants and place them in a plastic bag to go to a landfill.

According to the US Drought Outlook issued on June 19, 2014, half of Colorado is in some form of drought, with 15% of the state in a severe drought.[49] I only mention this because the geniuses at the Green Valley Ranch HOA have mandated their residents waste copious amounts of water on their perfect monocultures of grass.

Like many HOAs they mandate a "weed"-free lawn, which requires herbicides and increased water usage, in comparison to a native meadow. Unlike many HOAs they legislate against the dreaded bare spot, big or small! They also decree that you shall not have dry areas in the lawn either.

All right, this is insane. Residents are forced to create a monoculture lawn of grass that is hungry for water in a drought-stricken state. If the grass dies in even a little spot, they have to sod or seed the spot. That spot then has to be watered vigorously to establish the new grass. The only way these residents can abide by these rules is to irrigate these lawns throughout the summer,

48 GVR HOA, "Landscape Violation Frequently Asked Questions," *Green Valley Ranch HOA* (n.d.), www.gvrhoa.com/images2/doc/Resource%20 Center/Landscaping%20FAQ%20Sheet.pdf.

49 David Miskus, "Half of Colorado in Some Level of Drought," *The Associated Press* (June 23, 2014), http://denver.cbslocal.com/2014/06/23/ half-of-colorado-in-some-level-of-drought/.

when the earth in that state is especially thirsty.

What if you didn't comply with the rules? What if you received a complaint letter and you sent it back, telling the HOA president to stick it where the sun doesn't shine? What if you grew your front-yard garden complete with ten-foot-tall cornstalks and allowed your lawn to become a meadow of beautiful diversity?

Unfortunately, in most communities in the United States, you would find yourself in quite a bit of legal trouble. The longer you did not comply with their rules, the more fines and fees you'd rack up. Eventually they'd take you to court, and they'd win. If you continued to resist, they'd eventually put a lien on your home. Chances are they'd "fix" your landscape and send you the bill. They'd add that to the thousands of dollars in fines you'd already accumulated.

Jeffrey Demarco was cited by his HOA in Rancho Santa Fe, California, for planting too many rosebushes. Mr. Demarco balked at the complaint, and the HOA levied monthly fines. They then threatened foreclosure, and ultimately took him to court and won. Demarco was forced to pay the legal fees of the HOA totaling $70,000. He lost his home in the process.[50]

The Beacon Woods Civic Association in Bayonet Point, Florida, flexed their muscles when sixty-six-year-old Joseph Prudente, a retired registered nurse, failed to comply with the HOA's covenants that require homeowners to keep their lawns covered with grass. Mr. Prudente's sprinkler system broke, and his lawn withered and browned. The HOA sent him letters demanding that he resod his lawn by a certain date.[51]

---

50 The Week Staff, "Top 7 Insane Homeowners Association Rules," *THE WEEK Publications, Inc.* (December 15, 2009), http://theweek.com/article/index/104150/top-7-insane-homeowners-association-rules.

51 Jodie Tillman, "Brown Lawn Means Jail Time," *Tampa Bay Times* (October 10, 2008), www.tampabay.com/news/humaninterest/brown-lawn-means-jail-time/847365.

Prudente pleaded with the HOA for leniency due to financial hardship. His adjustable rate mortgage had adjusted upward for an additional $600 per month. Wachovia had repossessed his car, and his daughter and her two children had just moved in because they had fallen on hard times. On the verge of losing his home, he did not have the funds necessary to resod.[52]

Resodding a lawn is very expensive. A typical lawn of 5,000 square feet would probably cost around $5,000.

Prudente said, "To me, keeping the house is more important than the grass. I just ignored them."

I'm sure Mr. Prudente thought this nonsense would eventually go away. Unfortunately, it didn't. The HOA took him to court. The judge gave him thirty days to resod. A month later Prudente still did not comply, and the HOA was awarded $795 in fees. He had one month to comply or the judge would find him in contempt of court. Another month went by, and Prudente was found in contempt and ordered to jail without bail. Joseph Prudente was ordered to sit in jail until his yard was resodded.[53]

The HOA President Bob Ryan said, "It's a sad situation, but, in the end, I have to say, he brought it on himself."[54]

Let me get this straight, Bob Ryan. A man has brown grass, so that justifies taking him from his home and confining him to a jail? The "crime" of brown grass does not harm anyone. The crime of the kidnapping and confinement of Joseph Prudente certainly does. Criminalizing a nonviolent "offense" and responding to said offense with violence is immoral.

Prudente was finally released from jail, after his neighbors got together and "fixed" his yard for him.[55] The irony is that, after

52 Ibid.
53 Ibid.
54 Ibid.
55 Ibid.

they fixed the sprinklers and put in the new grass, the property is now worse for the environment than when it was "neglected."

The Tampa Bay Times citations in regard to Joseph Prudente are no longer available online. I did find the identical article reprinted on an alternate site. You can find that here: http://www.federaljack.com/brown-lawn-means-jail-time/. I don't know why the article was pulled from The Tampa Bay Times. I do believe in the veracity of the article despite the absence. Here's an alternate source from the Sun Sentinel.[56] It doesn't have all the details of the Tampa Bay Times article, but it does corroborate the main points of the story.

Homeowners associations are dangerous quasigovernmental organizations with the power to deny the constitutional rights of its members. If you think this is hyperbole, I suggest you read *Neighbors at War* by Ward Lucas. When you sign those HOA forms at closing, you are in effect signing away your constitutional rights to the whims of often immature, corrupt, and downright evil board members.

The famous Stanford Prison Experiment in 1971 demonstrated the capacity of cruelty in people when given power over others. One-third of the guards in the mock prison study exhibited sadistic behaviors during the six-day experiment. Most regular working Americans don't have the time or inclination to serve on an HOA board or even vote in an HOA election. This often leaves the power hungry, petty, sociopathic, and retired to run arguably the most powerful organization in the life of its members.

There will be plenty of well-meaning board members, but you are always one election away from tyranny—a cavernous topic

56 Barbara Hijeck, "Man Jailed for Brown Lawn," Sun Sentinel (October 13, 2008), http://articles.sun-sentinel.com/2008-10-13/features/0810140230_1_new-lawn-brown-lawn-lawn-police.

that would turn this book into a massive tangent. If you'd like to learn more on the topic, pick up a copy of Ward Lucas's aforementioned book.

If you're in the market for a home, I highly recommend that you purchase a house outside of any HOA. There is an erroneous belief that HOAs raise property values with their draconian laws. If people leave HOAs and refuse to buy homes within the HOAs' jurisdiction, these corrupt organizations will be exposed for the negative effect they have on a community and its property values.

My initial inclination for those stuck in an HOA would be to speak up and try to change the asinine rules, but, after reading *Neighbors at War*, I'm not sure it's wise. It is far too common for dissenters to be targeted by HOA boards. The stories of the targeted are chilling. It is not unusual for people to lose their homes over petty infractions. Even if you do battle with an HOA and win, you still lose, because the legal costs can be hundreds of times the cost of the original infraction. Meanwhile HOAs have insurance which allows them to hire the best legal teams.

The following is not advice. It is simply what I would do, if I were in an HOA. I'd sell my home as soon as possible. I'd rent in the cheapest place possible, while I saved up enough money to buy a piece of land without any deed restrictions and preferably outside any zoning restrictions. Once I had enough money for the land and a cheap trailer to live in, I'd move to the land and live in the trailer, while I built my home as I had the additional cash funds to do so. In this scenario, you have no worries about banks, interest, and how to keep up with the mortgage payment. This is the closest we can come to freedom in this country.

We need to stop being docile cows that fall in line with the herd. We need to start thinking for ourselves and standing up for what's right, even if it's against the rules, but we need to be smart about it.

- HOAs often criminalize "weeds," vegetable gardens, compost piles, and tall grass.

- Fines and penalties for having the audacity to disobey the mighty HOA can lead to foreclosure or even jail time.

- Even "good" HOAs are one bad election away from tyranny.

- If you live in a residence under the control of an HOA, get out!

Let's move on from other people's legal problems to my own.

13

LOCAL ORDINANCES AND MY LEGAL PROBLEMS

In the summer of 2009, Denise and I found a beautiful south-facing 5.6-acre property in rural Pennsylvania,
surrounded by farms, and with a great view. The property was
once a commercial orchard and, at that time, was being cut for
hay. We purchased the property and built a passive solar home
complete with a greenhouse, root cellar, solar panels, insulated
concrete walls, and geothermal climate control.

We purposely purchased the land outside of an HOA and in
a rural farming community so we'd be left alone. I had plans to
grow a large garden and raise some chickens for eggs and meat.
From 2009 to 2012 I mowed the pasture three or four times per
year. In 2013 I had plans to install a food forest, timber forest,
and a wildflower meadow. Therefore, I let the pasture, filled with
clover and alfalfa, grow a little taller than I had in the past to add
biomass and nitrogen to prepare the soil for the new trees and
wildflower meadow. My plans were about to be derailed.

In early June I received a phone call from a telemarketer seek-
ing donations for the police department. I was annoyed with
their use of intimidation to solicit money. The telemarketer used
a very effective propaganda technique called the fear appeal. Fear

89

The Author's Wildflower Meadow

appeals are effective because they divert our attention from careful examination of the issue to the fear itself—specifically ridding ourselves of the fear.[57]

According to Pratkanis and Aronson, "The fear appeal is most effective when (1) it *scares* the hell out of people, (2) it offers a *specific recommendation* for overcoming the fear-arousing threat, (3) the recommended action is perceived as effective for reducing the threat, and (4) the message recipient believes that he or she *can* perform the recommended action."[58]

The telemarketer said, "I'm Frank White from the North Lebanon Police Department." My stomach turned immediately

---

57 Anthony Pratkanis and Elliot Aronson, *Age of Propaganda: The Everyday Use and Abuse of Persuasion* (New York: Henry Holt and Company, 2001), 209.

58 Ibid, 213-214.

as fear washed over me. My fear was relieved when the man chuckled and said, "Don't worry you're not in trouble." The man went on to ask me to buy tickets to The Policemen's Ball.

I said, "No, you already get my money through taxation."

"Police officers risk their lives every day," the man said. "You want to support our dedicated officers, don't you?"

The telemarketer gained instant credibility when he said he was from the police department. He appealed to my fear by simply saying he's from the police. He immediately relieved my fear by telling me not to worry, that I'm not in trouble. This—as Dolinski and Nawrat demonstrated—made me immediately more compliant. When I said no, he used guilt to influence me by pointing out the ultimate sacrifice police officers make every day—the risking of their lives. I didn't buy any tickets, but I felt compelled to, and I'm sure they do quite well in their telemarketing techniques. It felt like a legal shakedown with fear and guilt that could be relieved with a simple purchase.

It may have been a total coincidence, but a couple of weeks after my decline of the telemarketer, I received a notice from the local police. The notice said:

> It was recently brought to the attention of the Police Department that the property you own, or occupy, is in violation of the North Lebanon Township, Ordinance Chapter 10, section 101, which covers the area of grass, weeds, and other vegetation. The ordinance addresses this area in part by indicating that grass, weeds, and other vegetation may not exceed **six inches** in height.
>
> It is the responsibility of the owner or occupant of the property to trim, cut or remove all grass, weeds, or other vegetation and maintain the property in that fashion. You

will have **seven days** from the date listed above to complete the work, or the Township may be obligated to take further action as outlined in the ordinance; this would include ongoing fines and possibly other appropriate action to bring the property into compliance; **the township will cut the grass, and a lien will be placed against the property.** This warning will be effective for **three years from the date of this notice.** No further warnings will be issued in regard to this ordinance, and future violations may result in a citation being filed.

I look forward to you complying with this request to avoid any future hardship. Should you have any questions feel free to contact me at the above number.

Sincerely,
Lt. Don Wengert

I had no way of knowing if the township police were targeting me or not. I would like to think not, but the timing of the notice concerned me. I wasn't aware that there was a law against having your pasture a certain height. I erroneously thought that I was safe outside of an HOA. The notice required the work to be done seven days from the date of the notice, which was June 18, 2013. I didn't receive the notice in the mail until the evening of the 22nd. They essentially gave me two business days to conform, or they would mow and place a lien on my property.

I have a complicated, interconnected design with ponds, swales, 2000 trees and shrubs, gardens, *hugelkultur* berms, beehives, chickens, food forests, timber forests, and a wildflower meadow. It would be impossible for someone to put a large machine on my property and know what to cut and what to leave.

They would inevitably destroy everything I've built over the past five years, then place a lien on my property, forcing me to pay for their destruction of my land and hard work. This bullying and forced conformity was not unlike the homeowner's associations that I was trying to avoid. The letter from Lt. Wengert said I should call him if I had any questions, so I did.

After I told him who I was, he replied, annoyed, "What do you want?"

I wisely kept my cool, and he softened as soon as I said the word "lawyer." I explained it was not practical to maintain six acres like a suburban lawn and that my property had been cut for hay for decades. He said that my property was waist high, and I needed to cut it, but he wouldn't be out there with a ruler. I got the impression that they wanted it to be shorter, but I wouldn't necessarily have to keep it mowed as often as a lawn. I acquiesced and mowed it.

By the following spring, I had planted more trees and shrubs throughout my property. Some were growing on the berms of my swales, and some were grown together, the makings of young forests. I planted a ground cover of clover, yarrow, dill, and chicory to provide nitrogen fixation, nutrient accumulation, and to attract beneficial insects. I mowed the ground cover a few times, simply to give the young trees some light and provide nitrogen fixation and biomass. The ground cover was typically a foot or so tall. I kept my pasture areas by the road mowed regularly. Other areas that were more hidden I mowed infrequently to allow more bee forage and wildlife benefit. I actually mowed more often than I had from 2009 through 2012.

Toward the end of July 2014 an old Chevy S-10 broke down along the busy road in front of my house. The owner of the truck pulled over just off the state road and parked it on my property. It sat there for a week and a half. I called the police and asked them if they could remove it. The officer told me to call a tow truck and recommended a company.

Apparently, because it was on my property, it was my responsibility. The tow truck driver was leery of removing the car, because he said that dirtballs who leave cars like that can come back and claim you stole something out of the car or broke something. He said I'd be liable. He said he'd talk to the police and call me back, but he couldn't guarantee anything.

To make a long story short, I pissed off the tow truck driver by calling the police officer to ask him whether or not they were going to pay for the tow. I never got to ask him that question because, as soon as I was transferred to an officer, he said they were coming out in half an hour. The tow truck driver said I made him look bad. The police officer seemed to think I was demanding that they remove the truck immediately, although he was very polite.

A few weeks later I received another notice in the mail about my grass and weeds that were too long. I felt like I was being targeted, and I was pretty pissed off about it. It seemed like quite a coincidence that, after each encounter with the police, a few weeks later I received a nasty gram. Thankfully Lt. Wengert had retired over the winter, so I was hopeful that the new code enforcement officer would be more reasonable. I called Patrolman Rick Kline and told him that I did not have grass and weeds that were too long. It was a living mulch and ground cover for a young forest. He seemed to be satisfied with that explanation.

Yet a few weeks later, I received another letter stating that I was violating the grass and weeds ordinance. The letter did reference our conversation, but it said that he would need to inspect the property.

The Author's Young Food Forest

I met with Patrolman Kline, and I was pleasantly surprised that he was friendly and respectful. I showed him around the property and explained the purpose of the long ground covers. I talked to him about the school groups I host and the benefit to my neighbors who used to be inundated with storm-water runoff before I installed the swales and trees.

He said, "Not everyone likes what you're doing."

He proceeded to tell me that they have one resident who drives around North Lebanon Township every year and takes down the address of every home in violation of the grass-and-weed ordinance. He then personally delivers the information to the police station. The police are then forced to enforce the rule. I argued that the rule is too subjective.

The ordinance states "Grass, weeds, and other vegetation may not exceed six inches in height."

I told Patrolman Kline that I could find grass, weeds, or other vegetation over six inches tall on just about every property in the township. He agreed with me and said he didn't have the time to prosecute, even if he wanted to. He also told me that, if there wasn't a complaint against me, he'd be fine with how I was maintaining the property. He thought my strategy of screening my property from the road with bamboo was a good one. As he was leaving, he told me that he would call me if there was anything I needed to do.

At this point I felt cautiously optimistic. A few weeks later I received another letter stating that I was in violation. I was disappointed that I didn't receive a call from Patrolman Kline ahead of time. I sent the letter to my lawyer, and he suggested that we appeal the decision. My lawyer drafted an appeal that read:

> Phil Williams recently consulted our office regarding the enclosed Notice of Violation dated September 11, 2014. The Notice alleges an ongoing high weeds violation. As permitted by your Notice, the purpose of this letter is to formally appeal this alleged violation. Additionally we kindly ask that we be afforded the opportunity to personally appear before the Board of Appeals in order to explain our defense to the suggested violation.
>
> As a brief explanation, we believe the suggestion of a weeds violation is misplaced under the specific circumstances of this case. Specifically Mr. Williams utilizes this property as an example of his expertise as a Certified Permaculture Designer.
>
> Permaculture design is a design science focusing on the development of land in a sustainable fashion, cultivating

natural habitats and food systems that are beneficial to both people, plants, and the local ecosystem. It promotes healthy reforestation and naturalization of land, and fosters the creation of habitats for pollinators through the development of wildflower meadows and emphasizes diversity in order to achieve a healthy food chain.

In short, Mr. Williams is fostering a natural, but planned, development of his land for the benefit of man and all other living organisms, and generally for the promotion of nature and its processes. Once again we kindly ask that we be afforded an opportunity to appear before the Board in order that we may further explain our unique situation in greater detail.

Ed Coyle, Esq.

I was again given seven days to appeal, which was really four business days from the date I received the letter. I had to schedule a hurried meeting with my lawyer, draft a letter, and hand deliver the document within four days. I went to the township office to deliver the letter, and the office staff sent me next door to the police department. I went next door to the police department and spoke with the receptionist behind the bulletproof glass. I told her that I had an appeal for Patrolman Kline. She looked confused, as if appeals were not a normal occurrence. As of May 30, 2015, seven and a half months after I dropped off my appeal, I have not received any correspondence in regard to my violation. I called Officer Kline in January, and he said they were planning a hearing in February, and that he would need to take pictures in the spring.

While waiting on my appeal, I've done further research into

the ordinance. The nasty letters from the police did not contain all the relevant verbiage. They left out a very important part. Below is the full ordinance from chapter 10, page 3, of the North Lebanon Township Ordinance Book. I highlighted and under-lined the important information they omitted.

Vegetative Growth a Nuisance under Certain Conditions.

No person, firm or corporation, owning or occupying any property within the Township shall permit any grass or weeds or any vegetation whatsoever, to grow or remain upon such premises so as to exceed a height of six (6) inches, or to throw off any unpleasant or noxious odor, or to conceal any filthy deposit, or to create or produce pollen. Any grass, weeds or other vegetation growing upon any premises in the Township in violation of any of the provisions of this Section is hereby declared to be a nuisance and detrimental to the health, safety, cleanliness and comfort of the inhabitants of the Township. **Notwith-standing the above provisions, these provisions shall not apply to those areas which are maintained, farmed, and used for agricultural purposes and to those areas when the Township is conducting recycling programs.** (Ord. 6/3/85, 6/3/1985; as amended by Ord. 1-1999, 8/16/1999, VI; and by Ord. 1-2007, 5/21/2007, X)[59]

How can you possibly ban plants that create or produce pollen? And what's the difference between *creating* and *producing*? My lawyer told me that the people who write these ordinances don't know what they're talking about. The police never mentioned in

59 North Lebanon Township, "North Lebanon Township Ordinance Book," *North Lebanon Township* (n.d.), chapter 10, page 3.

their letter that the ordinance doesn't apply to properties that are "maintained, farmed, and used for agricultural purposes." The ordinance does not apply to my property. Or at least that's what I thought.

The tyranny of the HOA is alive and well documented, but the tyranny of local government is growing. Zoning ordinances didn't exist in my township before 1984. Since 1984, virtually every year has seen an expansion of the rules that residents have to follow. Each year the *Zoning Ordinance* book gets a little bigger, and our freedoms are reduced incrementally with every rule they add.

A few years after my home was built, the builder told me about new legislation that requires the installation of indoor sprinkler systems in the homes he builds. An indoor sprinkler is something that has to be maintained and tested on a yearly basis, adding to the cost of home ownership, not to mention the fear of burning your dinner and setting off the sprinklers. You could ruin your furniture and carpets in short order.

The rules surrounding keeping animals in my township are an example of a vague ordinance that could be applied to everyone with an animal. As a chicken keeper, I am sensitive to the ordinances, because my chickens provide meat, eggs, fertilizer, insect control, and entertainment. In the North Lebanon Township Ordinance Book, chapter 2, page 4, the following rule is particularly nonsensical:

> Every keeper of any animal shall cause the litter and droppings therefrom to be collected daily in a container or receptacle that when closed shall be rat-proof and fly-tight, and after every such collection shall cause such container or receptacle to be kept closed. At least twice a week, every such keeper shall cause all litter and droppings

so collected to be disposed of in such manner as not to permit the presence of fly larvae.[60]

According to this rule, residents of my township have to pick up every last piece of crap that comes out of their animals on a daily basis and place it into a closed container, to be emptied into the trash at least twice a week. This sounds a lot like the ridiculous HOA rules that I addressed in the previous chapter. Can you imagine how bad that container would smell?

In my case, chickens produce manure constantly. They walk around and defecate. They defecate while they're sleeping. I move my chickens every week along the upper two acres of my property where their fertility is gravity fed to my trees. Even in the heat of the summer, they don't smell or cause any sort of nuisance whatsoever. They do scratch up the land and eat a lot of the vegetation, but, two weeks after I move them, those areas are fully recovered. I'd be willing to bet most dog and cat owners aren't following these rules. How many cat owners clean out their kitty litter every day?

What scares me the most about local government ordinances is that enforcement is complaint driven. Complaint-driven enforcement combined with rules that are cumbersome, draconian, vague, often contradictory, and growing by the year is a recipe for tyranny. I became a target for the police because someone went to the police station and complained about the way I was maintaining my property. This person does not have to prove damages or even be known to me. In this dynamic the police become Mommy and Daddy for the complainer. This gives immense power to the complainers of the township and no power to the property owners. I'm sure this control freak gets a <u>real charge out</u> of making the police run around and enforce his

60 Ibid, chapter 2, page 4.

vision of what others should do on their properties. It's sick that we cater to these types of people. I would have a lot more respect for the police if they would just tell this guy to get a life. People who know the rules can exploit them to force others to live the way they want them to.

In the previous chapter on HOAs, I warned about making yourself a target for reprisals by standing up and speaking out. My lawyer has advised me to conduct myself in a way that draws the least attention. Despite his advice, I've begun to attend township meetings. I was initially shocked at how few people actually attend. Apart from the people asking for permission to do something, my friend and neighbor Mark and I were the only people in the audience.

Watching property owners beg for permission to do something on their property was a stomach-turning event. One board member actually made a joke about how he liked to tell people what to do. The property owners were so docile and polite. *Please* and *yes, sir; no, sir*, with heads bowed, and a grateful "Thank you so much" when they were granted permission. This is not to say that I am any better.

There was a debate among the board over where $1,100 for ballistic shields would come from. The police chief was hoping the township would pay for them. One board member talked about the importance of "protecting our officers." Another board member agreed but thought the police could find the money in their budget.

I was thinking, *what the hell does the police department need ballistic shields for?*

Ballistic shields are used for riots. Police officers don't walk around holding their ballistic shields for protection in their normal routine. I wanted to ask, "When was the last time North Lebanon Township had a riot?" Instead I stayed quiet and docile, like my fellow property owners begging for permission. I know, like they do, that alone I am weak; that if I speak up, I may be targeted. If I'm targeted, the laws are vast and all-encompassing, nearly guaranteeing my criminality.

> *The only power any government has is the power to crack down on criminals. Well, when there aren't enough criminals, one makes them. One declares so many things to be a crime that it becomes impossible for men to live without breaking laws.*
> —Ayn Rand

Denise and I have already had conversations about leaving our home. I'm just not sure how long I can develop and live on a property where I am harassed by local government. The problem then becomes, where can you go? There are unincorporated places in the United States, not governed by ordinances and codes, but those places are in the minority. The majority of real estate in the States is governed by HOAs and/or local governments.

For now I'm planning to stay and make a difference in my community. Maybe my property can be an example to others of the beauty of working with nature, not against her. Maybe I can encourage others to stop treating Mother Nature like a slave to be controlled. We talk a lot about freedom in this country, but we don't recognize our own chains dragging behind us.

> *The best slave is the one who thinks he is free.*
> —Johann Wolfgang von Goethe

- Local government ordinances can be just as draconian as HOA covenants.

- My own local government has forced me to reconsider living in my community.

In the next two chapters I detail a single fictional community. In "A Tale of Two Communities, Part 1," the suburban residential community is run by an authoritative HOA. In Part 2, residents are free to live how they choose, outside of oppressive zoning ordinances and HOA covenants.

14

A TALE OF TWO COMMUNITIES, PART 1

It's 8:00 a.m. I'm roused by the roar of my neighbor's lawn mower. I roll over, pull my pillow over my head, and try to fall back asleep, but I can still hear that damn mower. I groan and throw off the covers and head for the bathroom. My wife frowns at me with a toothbrush lodged in the corner of her mouth.

"Does he have to mow *every* Saturday morning?" I say.

She raises her eyebrows and throws up a palm in commiserated frustration. Her reddish-blond hair is tied up in a loose ponytail. A few strands dangle in front of her symmetrical face. Her porcelain skin is tinted with strawberry hues. I stand in front of my sink, staring in the mirror. My hair is a lighter shade of brown than usual, and my tan has not erased the dark circles under my eyes.

Denise and I sit in silence, eating our breakfast of fresh eggs, strawberries, melon, and bacon, complete with the whizzing noise from a weed eater for ambiance. I glance at Denise, and she has tears in her eyes. She looks down at the kitchen table, then back at me. Tears overflow her blue eyes and spill down her cheek.

"I'm sorry," she says. "I know I promised I wouldn't make this more difficult for you." After a moment she takes a deep breath and furrows her brow. "This is absurd. These people are insane. How would Harold like it if he had to kill that dog of his? I'm going to go tell him what an arrogant ass he is!"

Denise stomps toward the side door. I shoot out of my seat and race her to the door, stepping in front, blocking her path. I hold on to her ... tight.

"There has to be another way," she says.

"We've been through this," I say. "I've tried everything, but we're out of time. If we don't comply, they'll fine us and probably foreclose on us, like they did to Sue. If we had the money, I'd gladly fight, but it was a stretch for us to get into this neighborhood, and, with dues going up, we just can't afford it."

"We need to get out of here."

"I'm working on it."

I exit the side door through the garage and smack the garage door opener. Our two cars are safely inside, because parking in the driveway is against the rules. The smell of lavender and rosemary emanate from my front-yard garden. I meander through the clover pathway. I can see the purple and orange tops of the carrots poking out of the ground, begging me to pick them. The tomatoes have onions growing around them as an insect barrier. The cornstalks stand straight, tall, and proud. Beans wrap around them, providing nitrogen to the hungry corn plants. Squash spreads out underneath, creating a carpet of green with thirty-pound crooked-necked pumpkins.

Honeybees, carpenter bees, and wasps buzz about, fluttering among the open flowers. Plump red peppers and shiny purple eggplants rise from the sea of orange marigolds, yellow dandelions, red clover, and white yarrow. Herbs are sprinkled throughout—basil and garlic near the tomatoes, and cilantro and oregano near the peppers.

I hear metal scraping and the whine of a small engine. I turn and see sparks shooting from Harold's lawn edger blade scraping against his concrete sidewalk. I look him in the eye. He looks down. Sweat beads roll down his red face and neck. The open collar of his too tight polo shirt reveals a bit of pasty-white skin. Cotton threads around his potbelly scream for mercy. His bright white legs match the skin at the point of his collar.

His lawn is dark green, completely uniform, with each matching grass plant standing in unison at perfect attention. The Aryan Nation would be proud of the lack of diversity. Corners are clipped and edged with precision. Planting beds are freshly mulched with neatly clipped, perfectly rounded shrubs.

I move around the house to the backyard. I see my moveable coop on wheels, with the little red hens foraging under the young food forest. They run up to me, expecting a treat. I stand motionless. They peep at me to get my attention, and pace back and forth along the fence in front of me. The largest hen stands still, turning her neck to look at me with one of her eyes. She squawks, then pecks one of the smaller birds on the neck for violating her space. I flip the switch on the solar power pack that electrifies the fence and step over into their pen. I crouch, and, within seconds, I'm surrounded. I pet a few on their back feathers. Some lightly peck at my shoes and pants, exploring for food.

I reach for the largest chicken, the head chicken in charge. She braces herself but is comfortable in my arms. I stand up, and she surveys her new vantage point. I exit the pen with the Rhode Island Red in my grasp. Her feathers are soft to the touch. She purrs and lightly peeps as I pet her. I walk to the side of the house, out of view of the others. The stainless steel cone is attached to a tree, with a straw-filled bucket underneath.

I gently turn her upside down. I can feel her heart beat faster. She struggles, flaps her wings, and peeps louder now. I place her headfirst into the steel cone. I take the razor-sharp knife from the outdoor table. I grab her head, peaking from the bottom of the cone, and pull it down, so her neck is exposed. I line up the knife under her ear, and make a long deep cut on one side of her neck and another cut on the opposite side, severing her carotid artery.

Warm blood immediately pours onto my left hand. She's quiet at first but then begins to squawk, a shrill noise. After twenty seconds or so, her body convulses. After a couple of minutes, she's limp, her blood and life exsanguinated. I put the knife back on the table and lean against the house. I slide down to the ground with my elbows propped on my knees, looking down. I feel a lump developing in my throat.

"Do you need any help?" Mark calls out, as he's walking toward me.

I stand and pull my sleeve to my eyes, wiping them dry. "Yeah, I'd really appreciate it."

"Today's the day, huh? And here I thought we had freedom in this country. What a joke."

"So much for our big garden plans," I say.

"I already bought the rabbit hutches. I'm glad I didn't get the lumber for the beehives yet."

A few hours later, I hand Mark his cooler filled with young tender chicken meat, sectioned and vacuum packed. As he leaves, I sit down on my cooler and hang my head. I hold my face in my hands. My stomach feels hollow, but I have no appetite. I close my eyes. I can still hear the squawking. I can still see the blood gushing from their necks. I can feel the warmth running down my hand. I remember the hopeful peeping, as I picked them up one by one. My chest and throat become tight. I have trouble swallowing. My eyes begin to water. I stand, not bothering to wipe the tears or the blood.

I hear banging coming from Joe's house, next door. I cross

Joe's asphalt driveway and head for the front door, where I see him trying to steer his wheelchair through the storm door, while leaning on his crutches. I hold open the storm door and pull the wheelchair onto the front porch. He hobbles around to the chair and slumps down, exhaling heavily. Joe looks like he'd fit right in with the Hells Angels, complete with an ever-present bandanna, Harley Davidson T-shirt, and a dark bushy beard.

"You look like you've been doin' some killin," Joe says.

I realize my face must be streaked with red war paint. "The chickens. I touched my face with my bloody hands," I reply.

"That asshole is lucky I haven't killed *him* yet."

"You look like you're getting around a little better."

Joe looks up at me. "I'll be in this goddamn chair until I'm dead."

"Joe, … come on. You don't know that."

"We should've been more involved. One of us should've run for HOA president, when Sue got married. Hell, we didn't even bother to vote."

"I never thought they could have so much power over us."

"Do you remember when he called the cops on me for brandishin'? That's when it all started. My Glock was concealed. The only reason he saw it imprinted on my back was because I bent over to pick up that goddamned beer can. After I punched him, it was like a slow bleed. They'd fine me for everything I did. If I worked on my bike in the driveway, they'd fine me. If I left a single oil stain, they'd fine me. Hell, they even fined me for havin' a red front door."

"I'm sorry, Joe."

"Yeah, me too." Joe looks over his steep steps. "I applied for permission to put in a handicap ramp. Denied of course." He closes his eyes for a moment. "There's not a day that goes by that I don't think about how I never would've worked those extra hours, if I didn't get those fines. I should've never been on that job."

"Let's talk to a lawyer. I can't imagine it's legal to deny handicap access."

Joe shakes his head. "It doesn't matter anyway. I'm gonna lose this house. I don't plan on seein' the end of this."

Silence engulfs us. I offer the only thing I can. "Would you like to come by for dinner tonight? Denise is gonna put something nice together from our last garden harvest. And we have fresh chicken."

"Sounds like a fittin' last meal." He gazes into the sun. "You're runnin' outta daylight. You should finish your work."

"I'll see you later on tonight then?"

Joe nods.

I stride to my front yard. I look at the walk-behind brush cutter that I rented yesterday, the big green monster. I put the ear protection over my floppy khaki hat and put my sunglasses on that double as eye protection. With one yank of the pull cord, the motor roars to life. Honeybees enjoy the yellow flowers from my broccoli plants. The tomato plants are loaded down with vine-ripened fruit. A few dozen watermelons aren't quite ready to be picked. My bell peppers are just starting to turn red.

I place the throttle on high, engage the blade, and place the machine in low gear. The machine slowly cuts its way through the junglelike paradise of edible plants and fruit. I try not to look at the plants and the bees as they're shredded by the machine. The brush cutter struggles a little with the dense plantings. On my final pass I turn around the machine, and Harold stands on my driveway with his arms crossed, wearing bright white socks and a triumphant grin. His salt-and-pepper crew cut and potbelly make him look older than his forty-five years.

I think that if I could get away with it, I'd kill him. The thought is not a passing fantasy. I had thought, planned, and fantasized about killing Harold in many different ways. I wish that movie, *The Purge*, was real. I bet people would be a little nicer to each other.

I look at his grinning face, and I lose all sense of reality. I put the Green Monster in high gear and start directly toward him. He's still staring at me with that same triumphant grin. I pass the edge of my garden, and I glare at him with the machine moving rapidly, a slow jog's pace. I'm twenty feet from him now, and my defense flashes before my eyes.

I didn't see him, Officer. I had on my earmuffs, and, when I turned the machine, he was there. I didn't expect anyone to jump in front of the mower.

His face is relaxed; his arms still crossed. As I get closer, his eyes widen, and his smile turns down. I know my face is caked with blood, and my eyes are wild. He's still standing on my property. I glance to my right, scanning for witnesses. I'm five feet away. I wait for the bloodcurdling screams of agony. I hear Harold yelp, as he's knocked to the side of the machine by the front caster wheels. His face is showing something I've never seen from him before: fear.

"Wait, wait, stop, stop!" he says.

I realize that his feet aren't the bloody stumps I had hoped they'd be. I whip the machine around and point it toward Harold, as he lay on the ground holding his ankle. He grunts as he struggles to his feet to avoid the Green Monster. He limps back to the safety of his property. I continue to guide the machine in his direction, property lines be damned. He glances back, as he retreats, limping across his driveway and along his sidewalk with the Green Monster nipping at his heels.

He opens his front door and slams it shut, as I run the machine into his door, creating a large dent. I hear the dead bolts latch.

I back up the machine and ram it into the front door one more time, deepening the gash. I turn the machine and take out a row of perfectly round hollies on the way to his sparkling white concrete driveway, where I do a few tight doughnuts, creating black tire marks in concentric circles. I see the hand-crafted wooden yard sign that reads Yard of the Month. I ram the posts, until they splinter, crack, and split. Then I drive the machine through my backyard to Mark and Desiree's house.

I bang on the side door with the machine parked but still running. Desiree answers, but I interrupt before she can speak. "Can I put this in your garage? If anyone ever asks, that's all I said."

I walk back home to face the music and wash up. I hear the sirens. I see the flashing lights shining through our windows, moving round and round on our walls.

"What happened?" Denise asks.

"I tried to run over Harold with the brush cutter."

Denise covers her mouth with her hand, her eyes wide open.

"Don't worry. He can't prove anything."

"Have you lost your mind? What are we going to do now?"

I hold her face in my hands and kiss her. "Please stay here. If they take me away, just meet me at the station. I love you. It's gonna be fine." I don't believe the last part of my declaration.

I exit the front door. Two officers force me down and bind me in handcuffs. I sit on my front stoop with my hands bound behind me.

"Your neighbor said you tried to kill him with your lawn mower," Officer Daley says.

Officer Daley is a clean-shaven, baby-faced jiggly mass of humanity, like an angry life-size version of the Pillsbury Doughboy.

"How could I possibly kill someone with a lawn mower? You'd

have to get him to lie down on the ground and let you run over his head. It's absurd. Take a look at my mower. It's in the backyard."

Officer Daley flags down his partner and tells him to bring the mower around front. The officer returns holding up the mower with one hand and a bucket of chicken heads in the other. The lightweight reel mower without a motor elicits a smirk from Officer Daley.

"That's not the mower!" Harold yells from his lawn, where he's making a statement to a female officer.

Officer Daley waves him off. "Sir, do you know it's illegal to slaughter animals in residential areas?"

"They're pet chickens," I say. "I had to get rid of them because my HOA was gonna fine me $150 per day if I didn't."

"That doesn't matter. You never should've brought them here in the first place. I *will* have to cite you for having the chickens *and* for the slaughter, not to mention this mess of debris in the front yard. You can't have debris piles in the front yard. On the bright side I do believe that you weren't trying to kill your neighbor with your mower." Officer Daley helps me up and undoes the handcuffs.

Harold screams at the female officer.

"Sir, you need to calm down." she says.

He pushes past her and stalks toward me. Harold yells, "You're gonna lose this house! I'll fine you into foreclosure. I guarantee—"

I hear the loud pop of a gunshot. The bullet enters the back of Harold's neck and exits the front, severing his carotid artery. The blood spatter is horrific, dousing Officer Daley and his partner in arterial blood. Harold grabs his neck, trying to stem the crimson tide. His legs wobble, and he falls to his knees, then slumps over on his side. The officers draw their weapons when they see Joe on the sidewalk in his wheelchair with his gun pointing in their direction.

"Don't shoot!" I say, just as the officers open fire.

Joe's body is riddled with bullet holes as the officers empty their magazines.

15

A TALE OF TWO COMMUNITIES, PART 2

I feel my body being shaken. I still see Joe's body slumped over in his wheelchair.

"Phil, wake up! Wake up!" Denise says, as she shakes my unresponsive form.

My eyes blink; everything's blurry. I can see a figure, looking down on me. I blink again, and I see her anxious face. A loose strand of reddish-blond hair falls down to her chin. I see her strawberry-hued skin, plump lower lip, and blue eyes. I reach for her and pull her tight to my chest.

"Are you all right? You were screaming, 'No, don't shoot,' over and over again."

"I'm fine. It was just a bad dream."

"What was the dream about?" Denise asks.

"We lived in this awful neighborhood with an HOA, where Harold was the president."

"That already sounds like a nightmare."

"I know, but it gets worse. Harold used his power on the HOA board to force everyone to conform to his vision of the community. Then anyone who rebelled became a target. Sue was evicted. I had to kill our chickens and cut down the garden. Joe was paralyzed in this horrible accident because he was overtired and working too much to pay his fines, and then he was shot dead."

Denise scrunches up her nose and frowns. "Sounds awful. By the way, your buddy is probably going to be at the picnic today."

"That's today, isn't it? What time is it now anyway?"

"It's past ten, sleepyhead."

I throw off the covers and leap out of bed. "I've gotta get going. I still have to pick the produce, and Mark and I were gonna harvest some fresh honey for mint tea."

"What about something to eat? We have tons of eggs and all those berries you picked yesterday."

After a quick brunch, I exit the front door with my array of willow baskets. I turn to glance at the yellow finches fluttering about the four-foot-tall chicory plants, looking for seed. I think about how much I love our home. The earth-sheltered one-story cobb home (constructed of clay, sand, and straw) complete with a green roof looks like we bought it from a hobbit. It's small but incredibly durable, energy efficient, and requires no maintenance. Apart from the front door and windows, it practically blends into the hill. We have a small carport that doubles as our solar array.

The smell of lavender and rosemary emanate from our front-yard garden, surrounded by a wildflower meadow of native flowers and common weeds. Bees and beneficial insects migrate to and from the meadow and garden. The whiz coming from Harold's weed eater destroys some of the peaceful ambiance. I put in my earbuds, with Alt Nation loud enough to drown out the noise pollution. I carefully walk through the garden on a meandering clover pathway, filling my willow baskets as I go.

The tomatoes are eight feet tall, on a wooden tepee frame. Beans use the cornstalks as trellises. Squash and watermelon are rampant, often covering the walkway. I step carefully, as I admire the abundance. I pick small yellow "lemon drop" tomatoes and large red "mortgage lifter" tomatoes. I think about how the productive meaty tomato got its name during the Depression by providing yields great enough to help pay a mortgage. I think about how my family's self-sufficiency and our back-to-the-basics living have kept us out of debt. I continue to move through the garden, picking peppers, eggplant, watermelon, cantaloupe, and zucchini.

I leave two heaping baskets of produce by the front door, carrying the others as I head to the backyard food forest to pick lettuce, spinach, broccoli, and kale. The cool-season plants do better with some shade in the summer. The young forest is filled with fruit and nut trees, as well as nitrogen-fixing trees. The trees sit up on berms with ditches behind them to harvest water and nutrients for the plants. The berms look like curvy waves along the contour lines coming down the hill. The ditches feed clay-lined ponds at each end.

The understory is packed with berries and large green leafy comfrey plants sporting purple trumpet-shaped flowers. I cut the comfrey periodically to provide mulch and nutrients to the fruit trees. I grow my summer lettuces in the open spots to take advantage of the dappled shade. I turn my head for a moment and I see a flash of white in my peripheral vision. My neighbor Harold frantically waves his pasty-white arms. I remove my earbuds and turn toward him.

"I was yelling for you," he says.

I walk toward him. "Sorry," I say. "I had my earbuds in."

He holds a spray can marked Weed Killer. His skin is bright white with blotchy red marks. His tight khaki shorts are pulled up about six inches too high, and the threads of his too-small polo shirt scream for mercy.

"I thought you should know, young man, that I've been

spraying your multiplying weeds all morning."

"You're five years older than me, Harold. Don't talk to me like I'm a kid."

"Well, I shouldn't have to clean up after you *like* you're a kid."

"If you sprayed that poison on my property, we're gonna have problems."

"Don't act like I'm the problem, mister. I'm sick of living next to your jungle. Let me show you what I've been dealing with."

I exhale and follow Harold to his front yard. His lawn is mowed incessantly to maintain a perfect uniform height of two inches. The grass is chemically treated to a deep green, without a single "weed," creating a Kentucky bluegrass monoculture. Corners are clipped and edged with precision. Planting beds are freshly mulched with neatly clipped, perfectly rounded shrubs.

"See?" He points. "Look at all these weeds coming up. I know they're coming from your yard. When you let those weeds get big, they spread everywhere."

I feel like the family dog that had an accident, with my owner rubbing my nose in the crap left in the living room.

"They're trying to fix your lifeless soil."

"My lawn's the greenest in the neighborhood."

"How much water do you waste? How many pounds of chemical fertilizers filled with salts do you dump on your lawn to turn the grass green? How many pesticides do you use every year to keep this unnatural monoculture? It may look green, but it's artificial. The soil life is dead, and I wouldn't eat anything that came out of your yard. Your lawn is the environmental equivalent of a heroin addict on methadone. Hell, I hope I don't get cancer from living next to you." I pick up a dandelion seed head.

"You need to fix this. You're ruining my property value. My next call is to the police if you're not going to do something about this." Harold shakes his fist.

"Go right ahead. There are no ordinances here. That's the beauty of freedom. You can't go around telling other people how to live on their own property."

A gust of wind blows the dandelion seeds into Harold's yard. He notices the seeds and cringes. "That's what I'm talking about. All those seeds make new weeds, which then make more weeds."

"That's the beauty of Mother Nature. She never stops trying to fix the damage you've done."

"It used to be people cared about their yards. Now I'm surrounded by all these damn hippies." Harold spits across the property line into my wildflower meadow.

"What are you bringing to the picnic today?"

"Salsa. Why?" He pronounces *salsa* like *s-owl-sa*.

"I wanted to make sure I didn't eat any poison today."

"Poison? The tomatoes are from my garden." He points to his six-by-six square plot framed with landscape timbers in the back corner of his property. "You're not the only one with a garden. You can have a neat property *and* a neat garden. You just have to work at it."

"I've gotta tend my chickens. By the way, later—when you're eating all that great food at the community picnic—remember most of that food is out of these messy gardens tended by dirty hippies."

As I walk back to the food forest where the chickens are foraging, I take a closer look at Harold's square garden plot. I wince when I notice the wilted tomatoes and peppers covered in white insecticidal dust. The understory is barren, without a single weed, and no mulch, simply cracked earth. I feel the urge to throw some compost and mulch on the dying soil.

I head over to the chickens. They pace back and forth along their fence, and peep in anticipation of their daily treat of kitchen scraps and damaged produce from the garden. I reach down and pick up the largest of my Rhode Island Reds. She braces herself when I reach down. She sits comfortably in my arms, purring. She looks around, surveying her new vantage point. I put her back down softly with her sisters. I open the old tin, housing the scraps, and spread the treats widely, so even the chickens low in the pecking order have a chance.

While they scramble for the treats, I open the nesting box and fill up my egg basket. A smaller hen finds some old bread and runs away with it, not wanting to share. The others give chase, thinking she should be more egalitarian. Once the bread is taken from her beak, the game continues until the tasty morsel is devoured.

After delivering the harvest to Denise, I grab my white zip-up bee suit and veil. It reminds me of a child's onesie. I pull on the suit over my canvas pants and gray T-shirt. The veil dangles off my collar, waiting to be zipped over my head. I shove the metal hive tool that looks like a mini-pry bar into my bee suit pocket. I walk through my backyard to Mark and Desiree's house.

Mark's property is even more junglelike than mine. He has large eight-foot-tall *hugelkultur* berms that double as windbreaks, creating many different microclimates. It's amazing how much produce comes out of the wood-core berms that never need fertilizer or irrigation. I see their eldest daughter, Emily, feeding the rabbits with some "weeds" pulled from the garden. The boys, three and four, run around the food forest, alternately hiding and chasing. Mark is suited up, his young face and jet-black hair obscured by the netting.

"Wait for me!" Emily says, as she bounds down the hill from the rabbit hutches, clutching her bee suit and veil. She's only twelve, but she's already five-foot-eight-inches tall, with lanky limbs and shiny chestnut hair.

"We haven't started yet," Mark replies. "Don't forget, if you get stung, you need to move away from the hive and let Phil smoke the sting. Those stings act like a homing device to tell the other bees who to attack, and the smoke obscures that homing device. Also, move slow and deliberate."

Emily puts her hands on her hips. "I know, Dad. I probably know more about the bees than you do."

Mark smirks and looks at me. "She's probably right. She spends all day learning with Desiree, and I spend all day at the body shop banging out dents."

Fully suited up, we approach the wooden hives strategically placed facing south, near one of my natural ponds. A wooden gazebo protects the hives from rain and snow. Evergreens are planted along the north and east sides to keep out the cold winds. The Warre beehives are six-foot-tall wooden miniskyscrapers with sloped cottage roofs. The busy bees create a collective hum. We take the roof and cedar insulation box off the hive. As soon as the insulation box comes off, I spray a little smoke on the bees. They retreat lower into the hive.

As we're carefully prying loose the top box of honey and comb, Mark looks at Emily and asks, "Why are the boxes sealed like this?"

"Because the bees use a sticky substance called propolis to seal their hive. This makes it easier for the bees to keep the right temperature and humidity, and to keep pests out," Emily replies. "I already know this stuff. I wanna have one of those bee beards that I see in my books."

Mark shakes his head. "Well, if you know so much, you should know why you can't do that right now."

Emily exhales. "Because they're not swarming."

With the box pried loose, Mark motions for Emily to pick it up. She removes the box from the hive, revealing honeycomb hanging from the top bars. She groans as she picks up the twenty-five-pound box. I smoke the box one more time. The remaining bees exit and head back to the hive entrance. Thousands of bees circle overhead. Emily carries the box away from the bees and sets it down in a wheelbarrow. I lightly brush the bees from the edges atop the hive before Mark replaces the cedar insulation box, cover, and roof.

"I don't think we killed a single bee," I say.

Mark looks at a cluster of bees eating honey from his glove. "They are docile. I guess we crush and strain the honey now?"

"Yep. I bet we have two gallons of honey in that one box."

On my way home with my family's one-gallon jug of honey, I see Joe in his driveway working on his motorcycle. His property looks like most suburban landscapes. The lawn is short and neat. He has shrubs and a few pine trees in front. There is an empty square of black earth surrounded by a two-foot-high wire fence.

"Hey, Joe. How are you doing?"

Joe looks up from his bike, his eyes just beneath the Harley-Davidson bandanna wrapped around his forehead. He walks toward me, holding a socket wrench.

"What's goin' on?" Joe says.

"Not much. Mark and I were harvesting some honey for the picnic."

"I saw you guys over there in your suits. I'd actually like to get a beehive. I was thinking about puttin' it over there," he says, pointing.

"That's a nice spot. There's a windbreak from the trees, and it would be pretty close to my pond, so they could easily get water. Are you gonna use your garden this year?"

"Nah. I don't have the time or the interest. Besides, everybody gives me so much produce that I don't need it."

"Do you mind if I start a few things for the fall in there? I'll give you half the yield."

"Have at it. By the way, I dumped a lot of grass clippings in your compost pile the other day. The pile's gettin' pretty big. Do you still want more?"

"Thank you, and, yep, keep piling it up. I'm gonna spread some of the finished compost in the garden and around the fruit trees next weekend."

"Did Harold talk to you yet?" Joe asks with a smirk on his face.

I laugh. "Yeah, we had a chat a few hours ago."

"He came over here earlier, asking me questions about whether or not I was pissed about how you keep your property. I told him to mind his own damn business. I guess he came to talk to you after that."

"He threatened to call the cops. I told him, 'Go ahead. There are no codes here.'"

"It really pisses me off when people try to tell others what they can and can't do on their own property."

"My brother lives in an HOA, and they can't even paint a door without permission. They had a neighbor who lost his home because he did some landscaping without approval. Now everyone's terrified to break a rule. I would *not* want to live like that."

"There's no way I'd let my home be taken by a bunch of self-important morons without a fight. I'd take down a few on my way out."

I laugh. "I don't doubt that."

"You and Denise going to the picnic today? The food forest y'all did in the park looks good."

"Thanks, yeah. What time is it anyway?"

Joe looks at his watch. "Almost one."

"I gotta get moving. I'll see you there."

* * *

Denise hands me the broccoli salad and mint tea she made. She adjusts her sundress, checks her hair, then takes the salad bowl again. She smiles at me. "This time it's not my fault we're late."

We walk briskly. I think, *luckily it's just a short walk to the community park.* At the entrance to the park, I show Denise the sign, Polyculture Park. Underneath the name is a list of all the neighbors who donated time or materials to the project. A food forest and a few ponds form a horseshoe around the park facing south. Inside the horseshoe is a massive community-raised garden complex for the nearby apartment and condominium dwellers. In front of that is a playground and sports field. The low-maintenance lawn is a mixture of clover and grasses.

When we arrive at the picnic, the park bustles with most of the neighborhood. The older boys play football. A few kids fly kites. The younger kids play in the playground. Two girls swing dangerously high, seeing who can go higher. Two little guys try to crawl up the slide, causing a traffic jam. Dogs circle each other and play-fight. Adults are scattered, some sitting on lawn chairs in informal circles, some standing in small groups, and some guarding the food from children's fingers and sneaky dogs.

I place our dishes on the wooden picnic table. I survey the chaotic scene. I see children and adults of all ages, shapes, sizes, ethnicities, and styles of dress enjoying a multitude of activities from the serene, intimate conversations to the thrill-seeking girls on the swings. I think about the beauty in our diversity but also the beauty in our similarity. It is our shared desire that binds us together, for our way of life to be respected and not infringed upon. We are all examples to our neighbors. If we want to influence someone, we show them a healthier, happier way to live. Good ideas don't require force of law or coercion.

I see Mark and Desiree standing with Joe, watching the kids. I see Harold sitting alone on his lawn chair. For a moment I feel sorry for him. I pour myself some mint tea with honey. Denise spoons some broccoli salad in a bowl for herself.

"Did you want some?" she asks.

I start to answer, but I see something disturbing. I see it all in slow motion. I feel a wave of déjà vu crash over me as my nightmare returns. Joe adjusts his heavy plate of food, and his unopened beer can slides out of his hand, bounces off his thigh, and tumbles to the ground. Harold glares at Joe, still pissed from their earlier encounter. I drop my tea and sprint in his direction. Denise watches in confusion.

"Joe! Wait!" I say.

Joe, already starting to bend down, stands back up and looks around. I dive on the ground, like the beer can is a fumble in the Super Bowl. My neighbors look down at me, dumbfounded.

"Are you all right?" Joe asks, half laughing.

Mark offers a hand to help me up. Joe smacks me on the back. Desiree, holding back a smile, asks if I'm okay. I hold up the beer can, celebrating my fumble recovery. I stop when I realize I'm the only one rejoicing.

"Oh, here's your beer," I say, handing the can to Joe.

He laughs. "You can keep it. You earned it. I'll go get another one."

If only we were all so lucky to live in such a place. Without suffocating rules placed on homeowners, the vibrant inclusive community I detailed above could be the norm. In the next chapter I detail how to live in a healthier, happier environment by doing and spending less.

16

LIVING HEALTHIER AND
HAPPIER BY DOING LESS

Throughout this book I've given the historical, cultural, legal, and psychological perspectives for why we maintain properties the way we do. I've made a case for why it's time consuming, labor intensive, expensive, unnatural, useless, divisive to a community, bad for your health, and horrible for the environment. Hopefully you're on board with me that we need to change.

This chapter is for those of you who agree with the premise of this book but have no intention of doing anything about it. You're too busy; you don't have the time. I understand. I don't expect people who read this to run out and become permaculture designers, ecologists, or naturalists.

In this chapter I'm going to give you a plan to improve your property by spending less and doing less. Here's where I make suggestions for what you can do, but, more important, what you can stop doing right now to make your little world, and by extension the big world, a bit better. My suggestions will vary, based on the type of community you live in.

If you have a company treating your lawn with pesticides, fire them immediately. You shouldn't pay to have your property poisoned. It goes without saying that, if *you* are the pesticide applicator, please stop. As bad as HOAs are, most do not mandate weed-free lawns, but some do. If you are in that unfortunate minority, talk to your neighbors about the heightened risks of cancer and autism in children when exposed to pesticides, not to mention the pollution of our drinking water.

Go to your HOA meeting with your cadre of concerned residents and politely reason with the board for a rule change. Notice I didn't say demand a change. In an HOA, you are at the mercy of the board. Be careful not to stick your neck out too far; it's bound to get chopped off. If you have an unreasonable board, run for office yourself or support a reasonable neighbor interested in doing so.

I think many Americans are obsessed with mowing their lawn. Mowing is ingrained in our culture. Think of the animated show *King of the Hill*, with Hank opening each episode on his riding mower holding a beer. Someone with an unmowed lawn is often thought of as lazy or sloppy. Meanwhile, someone who destroys bee forage, beneficial insect habitat, and wildlife, not to mention wasting fuel, is thought of as an upstanding citizen and neighbor. How often you mow, and how short you cut the grass, should depend on what you are trying to achieve.

If you're growing a wildflower meadow, you might mow once a season in the early spring, while the flowers are still dormant. This keeps succession from venturing past the herbaceous stage by cutting tree and shrub seedlings. If you mow more often, you'll short-circuit the natural seeding process of the flowers and cut many before they bloom. If you want to maintain a pasture, and don't have the animals to graze it for you, mowing a few times per season will encourage grass, and keep the pasture from being overrun with woody pioneer species.

Unfortunately, most of us would get into trouble with an

HOA or a code enforcement officer if we only mowed once or twice a year. For these circumstances, I recommend mowing as little as you can get away with—depending on the ordinances or covenants. In my township, it states that we cannot have any grass, weeds, or other vegetation over six inches in height. I've found this to be pretty common for HOAs as well, although I have seen other places that allow up to twelve inches in height. As you know from my earlier chapter on my legal issues, I have elected to challenge this rule. For the less foolhardy, I'd figure out what length your community allows, and I'd push that to the limit. So, if it were twelve inches, you probably wouldn't need to mow but once a month. Realistically, without rules to abide by, I think we could reduce our mowing frequency by two-thirds.

If you have a mowing service that you'd like to keep, ask them if they could mow every two weeks in the spring growing season, then back off to once per month in the summer and fall. This is for those of us with four seasons. If you live in Florida, this schedule would be different. This schedule would work well for communities that allow twelve inches in lawn height. Also, ask the mowing service to mow no shorter than four inches, so they don't destroy beneficial herbs that can't tolerate low-mowing heights.

If they can't do this, fire them and find someone who can, or buy a brush cutter and do it yourself. I recommend a brush cutter and not a regular mower because brush cutters can handle very tall grass, weeds, and even small trees with ease. Compared to a good lawn tractor, they aren't any more expensive. Most mowers that homeowners use will have a tough time handling the tall vegetation, making the chore of mowing very time consuming, even if it's infrequent. Raising the blade height helps mowers to pass through tall vegetation, because thicker vegetation exists lower on the plant's stems.

Walk-Behind Brush Cutter and Tractor-Mounted Brush Cutter in the Background

Don't waste water on your lawn. If it turns brown, that's fine; it's supposed to in a drought. The silver lining is brown lawns don't need to be mowed. Besides, the grass isn't dead; it's dormant. Grass plants allow the green foliage to wilt to save the roots. If the drought and heat are long enough, the plants can die, but that's fine too. Mother Nature will certainly send new plants that are more appropriate for the site.

If you're planning to hire a landscape designer for a project, consider a permaculture designer instead. People living on well-designed permaculture sites enjoy a natural abundance that I've never seen on a site designed by a conventional landscape designer. The best part is that, if you have little time, a permaculture designer can create the site in such a way that requires minimal maintenance once the system is mature.

Please stop with the crazy leaf cleanups. When you remove

leaves from under a tree, you're taking away the fertility and mulch that tree needs. Just let them fall and pile up. Yes, they'll kill the grass, but if you have enough leaves to kill the vegetation under your trees, nature does not want to have grass there. Other plants will grow in the understory. That's what happens in nature. What forest has grass growing under the trees?

If you just can't do this, if you spent your childhood, like mine, raking leaves, and now it's ingrained in your DNA, fine. You can rake the leaves but don't *remove* them. Blow them into a corner or an area that makes sense to have a compost pile. Pile them up, and they'll decompose over time. Please don't waste your life putting leaves in plastic bags. And for heaven's sake, don't remove leaves, then haul in mulch to replace the leaves you just removed.

Stop being so mean to your "weeds." They're just trying to help. Learning a little about the life cycle and functionality of common "weeds" can greatly reduce your weeding chores by allowing those plants to fill the niches Mother Nature designed for them. As an aside, I rarely remove the following "weeds" because they are so beneficial: clover, alfalfa, dandelions, oxalis, chicory, plantain, wild onion, henbit, chickweed, and yarrow.

Stop pruning your plants like you're Harry Homeowner Scissorhands. Plants aren't supposed to grow in neat little balls or perfectly squared hedges. Let them grow naturally. On trees the only pruning you should do is if branches are diseased, damaged, rubbing together, scraping along your roofline, crisscrossing, or growing back toward the trunk. And please, please, please stop hacking down a mature tree by 50% because you think it looks better smaller. The tree then forever forward looks awful, because you've hacked off its proverbial arms and legs. Severe pruning is acceptable when harvesting coppice wood, pruning out disease, or cutting back nitrogen fixers as part of a planned succession.

Stop throwing everything away. There is no reason to ever put organic material in a plastic trash bag. Start a compost pile for your leaves, grass clippings, and kitchen scraps. If the big bad HOA won't allow compost piles, use the Ruth Stout method of composting in place. Pull back the mulch, put down your kitchen scraps, and replace the mulch. The earthworms and soil life will do the rest and will thank you for it with healthier plants. In the particularly anal HOAs, you can use a mulching mower to return the grass clippings to your yard. The soil benefits from this, and you don't have to throw anything away.

If you can have farm animals, feeding them is the best way to get rid of kitchen and garden waste. They can take this waste and recycle it into meat, eggs, and fertilizer. Cardboard and newspaper can be used as the first layer over grass when starting a new garden with sheet mulching. I've taken thousands of square feet of cardboard from my local appliance store for this very purpose.

- Stop applying pesticides.

- Stop mowing so often and so short.

- Don't waste water on your lawn. It's okay if it goes dormant in the summer.

- If you're planning to hire a landscape designer, hire a permaculture designer instead.

- Stop raking leaves.

- Stop being so mean to your "weeds."

- Reduce waste by starting a compost pile.

The next chapter is devoted to those who have the time and inclination to work with nature to create beauty and natural abundance.

17

I WANT TO LIVE IN NATURAL BEAUTY AND ABUNDANCE

We need people to stop following the rules, to start break-ing cultural norms, to start pissing off their neighbors, to start building ecological landscapes that Mother Nature would be proud of. It's hard to be the first one in your neighborhood to go against the accepted norms of property management. You'll be much more likely to be fined, harassed, and looked down upon than if half the neighborhood were already doing it.

I hope one day we recognize the ignorance of spraying pesti-cides, keeping closely mowed lawns and weed-free landscapes without any useful plants. Until then we have to be the trendset-ters. We have to *do* what's right. It's not enough to talk about it.

The first thing I would highly recommend doing for anyone wanting to build and grow an ecological landscape is to take a permaculture design course, a PDC. I've taken two, read countless books on the topic, and practiced permaculture on my own land for the past nine years. There is no comparison between a perma-culture design and a conventional landscape design. It's shocking to me that permaculture hasn't taken over our landscapes, busi-nesses, and lifestyles. I suppose change happens slowly.

Bill Mollison, one of the founders of the design science, in *Permaculture: A Designers' Manual*, on page ix, wrote:

> Permaculture is the conscious design and maintenance of agriculturally productive ecosystems which have [the] diversity, stability, and resilience of natural ecosystems. It is the harmonious integration of landscape and people, providing their food, energy, shelter, and other material and nonmaterial needs in a sustainable way. Permaculture design is a system of assembling conceptual, material, and strategic components in a pattern which functions to benefit life in all its forms. The philosophy behind permaculture is one of working with, rather than against, nature; of protracted and thoughtful observation, rather than protracted and thoughtless action; of looking at systems in all their functions, rather than asking only one yield of them; and of allowing systems to demonstrate their own evolutions.[61]

PDCs are seventy-two-hour certificate courses that will give you the basics for designing a garden and lifestyle in harmony with nature. They can be taken online or in person. Geoff Lawton has a very detailed, informative online course that can be found at www.geofflawton.com.

At the end of the course, you will be required to design a permaculture garden. Most start by designing their own property, but I would highly recommend designing a friend's or neighbor's property instead. It's easier to be objective with someone else's piece of land. After you've completed the course, by all means design your own property, but, upon completion, I would

61 Bill Mollison, *Permaculture: A Designers' Manual* (Sisters Creek, Tasmania: Tagari Publications, 1988), ix.

hire a permaculture consultant to critique your design.

In a few hours an experienced permaculture designer could save you many thousands of hours of work by ironing out overlooked design flaws. If you don't have the time or inclination to take a PDC, but you still want that Garden of Eden, hire an experienced permaculture designer. A list of designers and their localities can be found at http://permacultureglobal.org/.

For those of you who plan to explore the exciting world of permaculture and to design your own paradise, I have some suggestions. Design the water first. Figure out how you're going to keep the water on your property for the longest time possible and how you plan to use said water. If you get the water right, everything else will fall into place.

It's really important to listen to the landscape. Don't try to fit a common permaculture feature into a design, just because you think it's ingenious. Permaculture designers use a lot of interesting techniques, features, and plants, but it's only ingenious because it worked on that site. It may not work on your site. For example, placing chickens in a food forest is a common design feature. The idea is that the chickens would forage in the understory and provide insect control and fertilizer. Unfortunately, they do not work well in young immature food forests, because they scratch at the roots of the trees and remove any mulch you may have applied. In my food forest, ducks are a more appropriate animal.

When you begin your design, simply observe and take general notes of what you see. Try not to think of what you should do. If you keep your mind open during the observation process, you will be more creative and accepting of ideas other than the preconceived biases we all have. A favorite designer of mine, Ben Falk, talked about how he wanted an orchard when he started to design his homestead in Vermont. He forced fruit trees into a wet area, and they died. Eventually, he settled on ponds and rice patties that were better suited for the area.[62]

Start small and don't be afraid to make mistakes. Good permaculture design is complicated, and practitioners never stop learning. I've rearranged my ten-thousand-square-foot garden three times. In retrospect, I should have started smaller until I had enough experience. I've tried different pathway styles, drip irrigation, wood mulches, living mulches, and hundreds of plant varieties.

Author's Mandala Garden, Fish Pond, and a Food Forest

Don't be afraid to ask for help. There are many great permaculture designers who will be happy to help with your design. It's better to ask than to make a type-one error. Paul Wheaton of www.permies.com once told a story of a PDC where he

---

62 Ben Falk, *The Resilient Farm and Homestead* (White River Junction, VT: Chelsea Green Publishing, 2013).

was teaching. A student proudly displayed a suntrap design. A suntrap is a horseshoe-shaped design with trees on the outside to trap the sun and create a warm wind-free microclimate in the middle. Paul turned the student's design upside down and said that it was backward. The student had his suntrap facing north, leaving the middle shaded and inviting for cold winds.

Asking for help isn't limited to design help. Maybe your design incorporates an earthen pond, but you have no idea how to build one. Hire a local pond builder. His expertise will be invaluable. Or maybe you have a thousand tree seedlings to plant, but your back is a bit old for that. Hire a local landscaper to help you out.

Don't be discouraged; everything takes time. Building good soil can take years. A mature food forest can take decades. I have trees that I planted five years ago that have yet to bear fruit. I have nut trees planted at the same time that won't bear a significant amount of nuts for another decade. When I first started developing my six-acre site, everything I did seemed like a drop in the bucket, but those drops add up.

My property has been dramatically transformed with 2200 linear feet of swales, 2000 multifunctional trees and shrubs, 4 ponds, 70 linear feet of *hugelkultur* berms, hundreds of pounds of seed, and hundreds of tons of compost and mulch. Six years ago, it was a degraded hillside cut for hay; now it is an interconnected, dynamic ecosystem brimming with life.

> *A society grows great when old men plant trees whose shade they know they shall never sit in.*
> —Greek Proverb

> *The best time to plant a tree is twenty years ago. The second best time is now.*
> —Anonymous

- Consider taking a permaculture design course.

- Don't be afraid to seek help.

- Water is the most important element in a permaculture design.

- Don't be afraid to experiment.

- Permaculture design is often slow and methodical. Be patient.

In the next chapter, I talk about the emotional, physical, psychological, and lifestyle changes that I've undergone over the past eight years.

18

THAT WAS THEN. THIS IS NOW. —S.E. HINTON

In 2007 my family, friends, employees, and acquaintances viewed me as an accomplished, successful businessman. My parents bragged to their coworkers and friends about how prosperous my company had become. It was easy enough to see. If you lived in the area, you often saw my shiny black trucks hauling mountains of materials, men, and equipment in and out of upper-class neighborhoods. I was the epitome of the American dream, barely out of my twenties, making money hand over fist.

It didn't matter that what I did polluted drinking water, caused cancer, wasted fuel, contributed to our shallow and materialistic culture, and created sad artificial representations of nature. What mattered to others was that I made *a lot* of money.

If you fast forward to 2015, I now live and work according to the three ethics of permaculture: care of the earth, care of people, and return of surplus. Denise and I grow and raise roughly 60% of our food intake. Each year our land provides a little more. Next year maybe we'll be at 65%. Even though I rarely buy material goods, outside of necessities, I want for nothing.

Our passive solar home produces twice the power it uses. The insulated concrete form home will exist long after I'm dead.

The trees and shrubs I've planted will be here producing healthy food and medicine far into the future. The ponds and swales I installed will continue to heal my land and the hydrologic cycle.

I now work as an author, activist, gardener, and permaculture designer. My income is a fraction of what it once was. I'm not the same person I was in 2007. I'm not interested in the same things. I don't watch sports anymore or much TV at all. Denise and I cut cable television in 2010, and we've never looked back. I don't know much about pop culture or local gossip. I'm not interested in having a nice car or wearing nice clothes. I don't own a watch.

Denise and I don't buy Christmas gifts for *anyone* because we don't want to contribute to the massive materialism of the holidays. We do give items from our homestead. One year we gave away dried basil and tomatoes. Another year we gave away seed and winter squashes. Another year, we gave honey from our bees.

It's a soul-satisfying sensation to have a job that nourishes you from the inside out. My endeavors produce the highest quality food possible for Denise and myself. My blog helps others learn how to design and implement permaculture projects on their own land. My permaculture designs, when implemented, become examples of ecological oases among manufactured, artificial landscapes. My clients, by extension, are healing their land and their local environment.

My career and life goals endeavor to regenerate degraded landscapes through permaculture design, while empowering and teaching others to do the same. Along the way something happened to me that was unexpected. While I was trying to heal the land, the land was trying to heal me. The simple acts of putting my hands in the soil, feeling the sun on my face, or picking ripe fruit has kept my depression at bay.

Today I would describe myself as content. I purposely did not use the word "happy" because, in order to feel happiness, you must feel sadness on the other end to know the difference. I certainly do feel sadness on occasion as well as joy, but my default emotional stasis is contentment, where it once was low-grade depression. I am extraordinarily grateful to be alive. This may sound like the fantasy ramblings of a pantheistic New Age hippie, but the idea that gardening cures depression is not without scientific proof.

Research has shown that contact with the soil bacteria, *Mycobacterium vaccae*, causes the release of serotonin in our brains. Lack of serotonin causes depression. Another study examined the dopamine release that occurs when food is harvested or found. This dopamine release produces a blissful state. The researchers theorized that the dopamine release evolved over 200,000 years, back to our hunter-gatherer days when discovering life-sustaining food would surely boost our ancestors' moods.[63]

I believe the rise in social, emotional, and physical disorders throughout the world can be closely linked to our increasing detachment from nature. We evolved closely with nature and all of her inhabitants. Despite our godlike technological innovations, they would not exist without the raw materials provided by the natural world. We must care for Mother Nature because our health, happiness, mortality, and all that we hold dear depend on it.

> *Though the problems of the world are increasingly complex, the solutions remain embarrassingly simple.*
> —Bill Mollison

> *All the world's problems can be solved in a garden.*
> —Geoff Lawton

---

63 Robyn Francis, "Why Gardening Makes You Happy and Cures Depression," *Permaculture College Australia* (2010), http://permaculture.com.au/why-gardening-makes-you-happy-and-cures-depression/.

19

UPDATE TO MY LEGAL PROBLEMS

In August of 2013, I was cited for having weeds in excess of six inches growing throughout my permaculture site. The rule stated that no weeds, grass, or other vegetation is allowed over six inches in height, unless the area is maintained, farmed, and for agricultural use. I was cited again in August of 2014. I appealed. I was granted a hearing in September of 2015. Below is a detailed account of the hearing.

I met with my attorney on my permaculture site forty-five minutes before the hearing. He walked the grounds, asked me a few questions, and we went over the evidence we had prepared. He reiterated to me that this was, "high stakes." He didn't have to tell me. I knew if we lost, I would not be able to continue with the permaculture site I had devoted the last six years of my life to.

On the way to the hearing, my wife Denise and I picked up two of our neighbors. Mark has the most adjoining property to mine. He's a good friend and also a permie; a definite plus for the good guys. Upon arrival, we loitered just outside the township building. A few friends and neighbors trickled in. The friends were mostly teachers that taught with Denise, but had also taken their students on field trips to our property. It was comforting to have supportive friends and neighbors, like stacking the stands of a football game with home team fans.

The room was setup with two rows of tables and chairs, with a space down the middle, forming an aisle. In front, there was a long table for the board and the township manager. Denise, myself, and my attorney sat in the first row on one side of the room, friends and neighbors sat in the tables behind us in the same row. The township manager, the township solicitor, and a young man sat in the long table facing us. The police officer sat in front in the opposite row, like he was from a different family at a wedding. The officer was built like a linebacker, his arms covered in tattoos. Shortly before the hearing was to begin, two middle-aged gentlemen greeted the officer with smiles and handshakes. I was concerned because I did not know who they were. Were they complaining residents?

The township solicitor told the middle-aged men to take their seats at the long table. At first I was relieved that they weren't complainers. Then I started to do the math. There were three board members, the township manager, and the solicitor. The township manager and the solicitor would *not* be voting on my fate. That left the young man and the two middle-aged men that were chummy with the police officer to decide my fate. I could see us losing two to one, before we pleaded our case.

The township solicitor started the hearing with the following statement. "This is the first time we've ever had a hearing disputing The Universal Property Maintenance Code."

The police officer presented his case first. He had pictures of my property from August of 2014 and more pictures from September of 2015. We received copies of the pictures. The police officer included pictures of other properties nearby with close cut grass and orderly landscapes. The officer described them as, "neat and clean." I leafed through the photos, and whispered to my attorney that I could explain the pictures.

The police officer went on to testify that in August of 2014 he received a complaint from someone who told him that he should check out my address because it was, "all weeds." He stated that he met with me, and I said it was a permaculture farm, and that I was getting a lawyer to appeal. In my opinion, his statements about our meeting made it seem like I was dismissive, and simply told him to back off. I did tell him that it was a permaculture farm, but I explained and showed him what things were, and why plants were tall. I talked to him about the mixed polyculture plants growing under my trees, and the clover and alfalfa living mulch. He went on to provide testimony that after I was cited, my property did not improve from one year to the next.

"I don't need a ruler to know that those weeds are longer than six inches," the police officer said.

My attorney questioned him about the specific wording of the ordinance. The officer referred to the Universal Property Maintenance Code that had been adopted in 2006 by the township. I had previously provided my attorney with the weed ordinance from the township's website. I was being cited with the weed ordinance from the Universal Property Maintenance Code, not the weed ordinance from the township's website. My attorney asked if they had two weed ordinances. The officer said they did. My head was spinning at this point. Our entire argument was that my property did not fall under the ordinance because it was maintained, farmed, and for agricultural uses. The Universal Property Maintenance Code did not provide that caveat.

My attorney began to present our case by asking me a series of general questions, questions he already knew the answers to. He asked my name, when we had purchased the property, and what it was used for before we moved in. It was a commercial orchard, then a hay field. The board asked me for a definition of permaculture.

I said, "Permaculture is a design science that seeks to design and implement self-sustaining and regenerative systems that provide for human, plant, and wildlife needs. Permaculture is guided by three ethics: care of the earth, care of people, and return of surplus."

"Where did that definition come from?" the stocky, balding board member on the left asked.

"I made it up," I replied.

He frowned.

"If you google permaculture defined, you'll find many different definitions and variations of the definition I gave. I think the one I provided is a good one based on my work and study in the field."

"Is permaculture defined in Webster's Dictionary?"

"I don't think so, but I've never looked it up."

My attorney asked me to stand and approach the board. He had the officer's pictures in hand. The police officer was also standing in front of the board. My attorney asked me questions about each of the officer's pictures. I explained the concept of a forest garden, and the purpose of living mulch. Most of the officer's pictures were from my zone 1 garden, which is weeded heavily. Granted it looks lush and overgrown, but if you know plants, you'd recognize most things.

The police officer pointed to a vine in the picture. "What's this?"

"It's a grape vine," I replied.

The police officer pointed to an enormous grass. "What's this?"

"Don't answer that," my attorney said.

"It's Miscanthus sinesis, an ornamental grass," I said.

My attorney submitted our own color photos in a binder for evidence. I had prepared captions for each photo. The first picture was a polyculture fruit tree guild in front of my fish pond. It was a plum tree, with oregano, comfrey, autumn olive, milkweed, alfalfa, clover, and nanking cherry growing in the understory. I explained to the board the concept of cooperative plant guilds. I flipped the page of the binder and two pictures were revealed. One showed a skid-steer dumping clay into the keyway of my future fish pond, the next showed the pond filling in the rain.

"Did you get a permit for that pond?" the stocky board member on the left asked.

"I did. I had to provide a drawing and pay $300, and they never even showed up," I replied.

"That wasn't us," the female township manager said.

"I know, it was the County Conservation District."

I turned the page again, and the next photo showed the pond more mature, with cattails bursting from the water. I explained to the board that without the water plants, the pond would be overtaken with algae. The next photo was taken from my bathroom window, and showed swales, three ponds, a young food forest, and an older food forest. My attorney asked a few pointed questions about the living mulch under the trees.

"Is there any grass longer than six inches in height under those trees?" the board member on the left asked.

"Yes, but it's impractical to mow," I replied.

"It's difficult for everyone." He frowned and pointed at the picture of my food forest. "Are you growing a forest or a garden?"

They seemed to have an issue with growing a forest. "Call it what you want, but I do harvest food from it."

"Do you *ever* mow under the trees?"

"A few times when the trees were small to keep the clover

from shading them out. I don't anymore."

"Then you have grass over six inches in height."

"Yes, but if I mow constantly, the only thing that survives is the grass. All the helpful guild plants don't tolerate frequent close mowing."

"Have you had any complaints from your direct neighbors?" the board member asked.

"No."

"It was just a busy body, then." He paused for a moment. "The people in the audience, are they neighbors?"

"Yes."

The board then allowed each of my friends and neighbors to speak one by one. I had a lump in my throat as they each detailed in their own way how they loved what we were doing and felt it was a benefit to the community.

After the audience spoke, my attorney flipped another page in the binder and asked me what was depicted.

"It's our wildflower meadow," I replied.

The board members barely glanced at it.

The member on the left said, "I was on the other side, but he convinced me. I've seen enough. I'm ready to vote in favor of Mr. Williams."

The other board members concurred. It was over. We won.

Denise and I shook hands with everyone and thanked our friends and neighbors. Outside, I thanked my attorney.

On the way to the car, my friend Mark grabbed me by the shoulders for a moment, and with a big smile he said, "You did it. How do you feel?"

"I'm not sure," I replied.

When Denise and I got home, I had mixed emotions. On the one hand, I was happy and relieved to have the weight of the township off my back, but on the other hand I felt empty and powerless. I knew how little power I had. I knew that everything I had worked for could've been taken by a single complaint. I'm sure the government officials in the room thought I should be grateful for their understanding. I felt sad that I had to fight for the right to care for people and the earth. I felt sad that the default legally accepted property management is one of dominance, pollution, and exploitation.

A few days later, my attorney sent me the following letter.

Dear Mr. & Mrs. Williams:

I appreciated the opportunity to visit your property prior to the hearing. It was a most enlightening half hour.

I am glad that last night we were able to remove the fate that has been hanging over your head in regard to the work that you have done on your property.

I complement both of you on your efforts to have people come to the hearing to support you. Their presence was very important. If you do talk to them, please express my appreciation for them being there.

The candor and forthrightness which you exhibited to the Board convinced them that the imposition of silly language from an International Property Maintenance Code has no applicability to your home and the project that you are undertaking.

It is most unusual and, quite frankly, I cannot remember a time when in the middle of a hearing a Board who started out being totally against a project, in the middle of the presentation, decided to call it quits and tell you that you are correct. You should take that as a high compliment.

I am sure that from time to time I will come out and meander through your facility. Please don't get your bees after me.

I have not read your book, *Fire the Landscaper*, but do intend to read it. Last night, I did however pick up a quote on page 133. "Society grows great when old men plant trees whose shade they know they shall never sit in." How applicable that is, not only to your landscape but to life and society in general.

Shortly after the hearing, Denise and I invited our friends and neighbors over for a celebration cookout. Denise named it the "Legal Weed Party." Everyone showed up that Saturday with their spouses and children. We ate homemade vegetable soup with all the ingredients coming from our garden. We had two pots, one with beef from our neighbor's cattle, and the other for the vegetarians. We had locally made bread. We had apples from our trees, with honey from the bees for dessert. Mark and Desiree's boys helped me harvest some ripe plums. Their reward was instant and delicious.

When Denise and I moved here in 2009, our property was a degraded hay field. We didn't have any friends. Mark and Desiree became great friends because we brought them eggplant from our garden. We buy beef from Sue and Dennis, but they became friends because of our shared love of farming. Joe's a great guy. He doesn't garden, but he supports our right to do so, and if you ever need some obscure tool, he has it. Adam and Tina have a wonderful young family and gardening is usually a topic of conversation.

I met Mahmoud when he was picking wild Mustard along the roadside. He now has a garden plot on my property. He told me that I'm the only American born friend he has.

Denise and I live in an oasis of life and beauty and abundance. I've put thousands of hours of hard work into this land, but it's given back far more. It's cured me of depression. It's given me food and medicine. It's given me friends and community. It's given me purpose. Most importantly, my connection with this land has connected me with Mother Nature and all her inhabitants. I believe it's this connection that human beings need to be human to the earth and each other.

Your To-Do and To-Don't Recap

We're all at different stations in our lives, but do what you can with what you have. Here are the main ideas I've discussed herein, put in an easy-to-read bulleted list. Pick one you can begin doing today. Review the list often and keep adding more into your daily life.

- Learn about the benefits of common garden "weeds" and stop removing and killing them with herbicide.

- Grow plants in diverse plant communities called polycultures. Try to stay away from single-plant monocultures.

- You can't control everything, so don't try. Your landscape doesn't have to be in perfect order; it's unnatural.

- Trying working according to natural principles. Remember, if we try to go against Mother Nature, she'll never tire in fixing our errors.

- Stop spraying pesticides on your lawn and landscape, and certainly don't hire someone to do so.

- Try to save and use as much of the water that comes to your site as possible.

- If you are going to hire a landscape designer, hire a permaculture designer instead.

- Don't mow so often and so short.

- Don't bother removing leaves; let them nourish the trees.

- Before you buy residential property, see if there's an HOA. If so, buy elsewhere.

- If you already live in a residential area with an HOA, look for a new place to live that has no HOA.

- Consider taking a permaculture design course.

- Grow your own food.

- Take action in your own community to reduce the ordinances and covenants that restrict gardening and permaculture.

- Work with nature to create your own permaculture oasis of beauty and abundance.

Succession in Pictures

The following pictures are from my property via Google Earth.

Dear Reader,

I'm thrilled that you took precious time out of your life to read my book. Thank you! I hope you found it entertaining, engaging, and thought-provoking. As an activist for nature and a small businessman, I only succeed if others take notice and *do* something. In the endless sea of e-books, it's easy to get lost in the fray. One way my message can be spread is with a positive review on Amazon. The more five-star reviews I receive, the more my book will vault up the sales charts. I would be immensely grateful if you would write a review. It doesn't need to be long and detailed, if you're more of a reader than a writer.

If you're interested in receiving my novel Against the Grain for free and/or reading my other titles for free or discounted, go to the following link: http://www.PhilWBooks.com. You're probably thinking, What's the catch? There is no catch.

If you want to contact me, don't be bashful. I can be found at Phil@PhilWBooks.com. I do my best to respond to all emails.

Sincerely,
Phil M. Williams

P.S.- May your lawn be forever long, filled with "weeds" and bees, pesticide-free, and brimming with life!

References

Ba nerjee, Neela. "Georgia Officials Give Drought the Silent Treatment." *Los Angeles Times* (September 16, 2012). http://articles.latimes.com/2012/sep/16/nation/la-na-georgia-drought-20120916.

Beyond Pesticides. (n.d.). https://beyondpesticides.org/resources/pesticide-gateway.

Bostock, Mike, Kevin Quealy. "Mapping the Spread of Drought across the US." *The New York Times Company* (April 9, 2015). www.nytimes.com/interactive/2014/upshot/mapping-the-spread-of-drought-across-the-us.html?_r=0&abt=0002&abg=0.

"Colony Collapse Disorder Progress Report." *USDA* (June 2010). https://www.ars.usda.gov/is/br/ccd/ccdprogressreport2010.pdf.

Falk, Ben. *The Resilient Farm and Homestead*. White River Junction, VT: Chelsea Green Publishing, 2013.

Fish, J. "Lawn Madness: The Tyranny of Greenery." *The Epoch USA, Inc.* (April 17, 2008). www.theepochtimes.com/news/8-4-17/68969.html.

Francis, Robyn. "Why Gardening Makes You Happy and Cures Depression." *Permaculture College Australia* (2010). http://permaculture.com.au/why-gardening-makes-you-happy-and-cures-depression/.

Gilliom, R., P. Hamilton. "Pesticides in the Nation's Streams and Groundwater, 1992-2001: A Summary." *US Geological Survey* (March 2006). http://pubs.usgs.gov/fs/2006/3028/.

Gleick, Peter H. *Water in Crisis: A Guide to the World's Freshwater Resources.* Oxford, UK: Oxford University Press, 1993.

GVR HOA. "Landscape Violation Frequently Asked Questions." *Green Valley Ranch HOA* (n.d.). www.gvrhoa.com/images2/doc/Resource%20Center/Landscaping%20FAQ%20Sheet.pdf.

Hemenway, Toby. *Gaia's Garden: A Guide to Home-Scale Permaculture.* White River Junction, VT: Chelsea Green Publishing, 2009.

Henry, Mickael, et al. "A Common Pesticide Decreases Foraging Success and Survival in Honeybees." *Science* (April 20, 2012). http://science.sciencemag.org/content/336/6079/348.

Hijeck, Barbara. "Man Jailed for Brown Lawn." *Sun Sentinel* (October 13, 2008). http://articles.sun-sentinel.com/2008-10-13/features/0810140230_1_new-lawn-brown-lawn-lawn-police.

Jenkins, Virginia S. *The Lawn: A History of an American Obsession.* Washington, DC: Smithsonian Books, 1994.

Kaiman, Jonathan. "Chinese Environment Official Challenged to Swim in Polluted River." *Guardian*

News and Media United (February 21, 2013). www. theguardian.com/environment/2013/feb/21/ chinese-official-swim-polluted-river.

Konkel, Lindsey. "Autism Risk Higher Near Pesticide-Treated Fields, Study Says." *Environmental Health Sciences* (June 23, 2014). www.environmentalhealthnews.org/ehs/ news/2014/jun/autism-and-pesticides.

LaVista, Jennifer, Leslie Desimone. "Contamination in US Private Wells." *US Geological Survey* (March 2009). http:// water.usgs.gov/edu/gw-well-contamination.html.

"Lawn." *Wikipedia* (n.d.). http://en.wikipedia.org/wiki/Lawn.

"List of Highest-Income Counties in the United States." *Wikipedia* (2014). http://en.wikipedia.org/wiki/ List_of_highest-income_counties_in_the_United_States.

Lucas, Ward. *Neighbors at War: The Creepy Case against Your Homeowners Association*. Morrison, CO: Hogback Publishing, 2012.

Malewitz, Jim. "Ogallala Aquifer in Focus as Drought Ravages High Plains States." *HPMG News* (March 18, 2013). www.huffingtonpost.com/2013/03/18/ogallala-aquifer- drought_n_2902037.html.

Miller, Frederic P. *Confirmation Bias*. Saarbrucken, Germany: VDM Publishing, 2009.

"Milorganite." *Wikipedia* (2018). https://en.wikipedia.org/wiki/ Milorganite.

Miskus, David. "Half of Colorado in Some Level of Drought." *The Associated Press* (June 23, 2014). http://denver.cbslocal .com/2014/06/23/half-of-colorado-in-some-level-of-drought/.

Mollison, Bill. *Permaculture: A Designers' Manual*. Sisters

Creek, Tasmania: Tagari Publications, 1988.

Molyneux, Stefan. *Free domain radio* (2005-2014). https://freedomainradio.com/.

Nielsen, Susan Searles, et al. "Childhood Brain Tumors, Residential Insecticide Exposure, and Pesticide Metabolism Genes." *Beyond Pesticides* (January 2010). https://ehp.niehs.nih.gov/0901226/.

Nolan, Bernard, et al. "A National Look at Nitrate Contamination of Groundwater." *US Geological Survey* (August 31, 1997). http://water.usgs.gov/nawqa/nutrients/pubs/wcp_v39_no12/.

North Lebanon Township. "North Lebanon Township Ordinance Book." *North Lebanon Township* (n.d.). https://ecode360.com/NO1608.

Organic Gardening. "Organic Fertilizers." (n.d.). www.organicgardening.com/learn-and-grow/organic-fertilizers.

Payne, Emily. "Is Sin City about to Run Dry?" *Associated Newspapers LTD.* (July 1, 2014). www.dailymail.co.uk/travel/article-2676186/Is-Sin-City-run-dry-Las-Vegas-danger-running-water-14-year-drought.html.

Pratkanis, Anthony and Elliot Aronson. *Age of Propaganda: The Everyday Use and Abuse of Persuasion* (New York: Henry Holt and Company, 2001).

Ritter, K. "Southwest Braces as Lake Mead Water Levels Drop." *Associated Press* (August 8, 2014). http://bigstory.ap.org/article/southwest-braces-lake-mead-water-levels-drop.

Rowe, Jack. "Trees and the Water Cycle." *Permaculture and Sanity* (n.d.). http://permaculture-and-sanity.com/pcarticles/trees-and-the-water-cycle.php.

Saier Jr, Milton H. "Desertification and Migration." *Water, Air, and Soil Pollution* (June 6, 2007). https://link.springer. com/article/10.1007/s11270-007-9429-6.

"Stanford Prison Experiment." *Wikipedia* (n.d.). http:// En.wikipedia.org/wiki/Stanford_prison_experiment.

Steinberg, Ted. *American Green: The Obsessive Quest for the Perfect Lawn.* New York, NY: W.W. Norton & Co., 2006.

Stevens, Jane E. "What's Your ACE Score?" (November 2011). http://acestoohigh.com/got-your-ace-score/.

Stout, Martha. *The Sociopath Next Door.* New York, NY: Broadway Books, 2005.

Tan, Monica. "Over One-Third of Rural China Lacks Access to Clean Drinking Water." *Greenpeace* (March 29, 2012). www.greenpeace.org/eastasia/news/blog/ over-one-third-of-rural-china-lack-access-to-/ blog/39721/.

Teitelbaum, Susan, et al. "Reported Residential Pesticide Use and Breast Cancer Risk on Long Island, New York." *American Journal of Epidemiology* (December 13, 2006). http://epiville.ccnmtl.columbia.edu/assets/pdfs/ Stellman%20pesticide%20breast%20cancer-1.pdf.

"The Quality of Our Nation's Water." *Environmental Protection Agency* (1998). https://www.epa.gov/sites/production/ files/2015-09/documents/1998_national_water_quality_ inventory_report_to_congress.pdf.

The Week Staff. "Top 7 Insane Homeowners Association Rules." *THE WEEK Publications, Inc.* (December 15, 2009). http://theweek.com/article/index/104150/ top-7-insane-homeowners-association-rules.

Tillman, Jodie. "Brown Lawn Means Jail Time." *Tampa Bay Times* (October 10, 2008). www.tampabay.com/news/humaninterest/brown-lawn-means-jail-time/847365.

"Tristate Water Dispute." *Wikipedia* (n.d.). http://En.wikipedia.org/wiki/Tri-state_water_dispute.

"UN Water factsheet on water security." *UN Water* (2006). www.un.org/waterforlifedecade/scarcity.shtml.

Wessex HOA. "Wessex HOA Lawn and Garden Maintenance Guidelines." (n.d.). www.wessexhoa.org/pdfs/Wessex_HOA_Annual__Lawn_and_Garden_Maintenance_Guidelines.pdf.

"What Is Groundwater?" *US Geological Survey* (January 1, 2014). http://pubs.usgs.gov/of/1993/ofr93-643/.

Willbrooke HOA. "Yard Care Rules and Regulations." (n.d.). www.willbrooke.org/covenants/Yardcarerequirementsfinalrevised.pdf.